THE LEGEND OF JUBAL AND OTHER POEMS.

THE LEGEND OF JUBAL AND OTHER POEMS.

BY

GEORGE ELIOT.

AUTHOR'S EDITION.

BOSTON:
JAMES R. OSGOOD AND COMPANY,
(LATE TICKNOR & FIELDS, AND FIELDS, OSGOOD, & CO.)
1874.

[*FROM ADVANCE SHEETS.*]

BOSTON:
RAND, AVERY, & CO., ELECTROTYPERS AND PRINTERS,
117 FRANKLIN STREET.

THE

LEGEND OF JUBAL

AND OTHER POEMS.

BY

GEORGE ELIOT.

AUTHOR'S EDITION.

BOSTON:
JAMES R. OSGOOD AND COMPANY,
(LATE TICKNOR & FIELDS, AND FIELDS, OSGOOD, & CO.)
1874.

[*FROM ADVANCE SHEETS.*]

BOSTON:
RAND, AVERY, & CO., ELECTROTYPERS AND PRINTERS,
117 FRANKLIN STREET.

CONTENTS.

THE LEGEND OF JUBAL.

THE LEGEND OF JUBAL.

When Cain was driven from Jehovah's land
He wandered eastward, seeking some far strand
Ruled by kind gods who asked no offerings
Save pure field-fruits, as aromatic things,
To feed the subtler sense of frames divine
That lived on fragrance for their food and wine:
Wild joyous gods, who winked at faults and folly,
And could be pitiful and melancholy.
He never had a doubt that such gods were;
He looked within, and saw them mirrored there.
Some think he came at last to Tartary,
And some to Ind; but, howsoe'er it be,
His staff he planted where sweet waters ran,
And in that home of Cain the Arts began.

Man's life was spacious in the early world:
It paused, like some slow ship with sail unfurled
Waiting in seas by scarce a wavelet curled;
Beheld the slow star-paces of the skies,
And grew from strength to strength through centuries;
Saw infant trees fill out their giant limbs,
And heard a thousand times the sweet birds' marriage hymns.

In Cain's young city none had heard of Death
Save him, the founder; and it was his faith
That here, away from harsh Jehovah's law,
Man was immortal, since no halt or flaw
In Cain's own frame betrayed six hundred years,
But dark as pines that autumn never sears
His locks thronged backward as he ran, his frame
Rose like the orbèd sun each morn the same,
Lake-mirrored to his gaze; and that red brand,
The scorching impress of Jehovah's hand,
Was still clear-edged to his unwearied eye,
Its secret firm in time-fraught memory.

He said, " My happy offspring shall not know
That the red life from out a man may flow
When smitten by his brother." True, his race
Bore each one stamped upon his new-born face
A copy of the brand no whit less clear;
But every mother held that little copy dear.

Thus generations in glad idlesse throve,
Nor hunted prey, nor with each other strove;
For clearest springs were plenteous in the land,
And gourds for cups; the ripe fruits sought the hand,
Bending the laden boughs with fragrant gold;
And for their roofs and garments wealth untold
Lay everywhere in grasses and broad leaves:
They labored gently, as a maid who weaves
Her hair in mimic mats, and pauses oft
And strokes across her hand the tresses soft,
Then peeps to watch the poisèd butterfly,
Or little burthened ants that homeward hie.
Time was but leisure to their lingering thought,
There was no need for haste to finish aught;

But sweet beginnings were repeated still
Like infant babblings that no task fulfil;
For love, that loved not change, constrained the
simple will.

Till, hurling stones in mere athletic joy,
Strong Lamech struck and killed his fairest boy,
And tried to wake him with the tenderest cries,
And fetched and held before the glazèd eyes
The things they best had loved to look upon;
But never glance or smile or sigh he won.
The generations stood around those twain
Helplessly gazing, till their father Cain
Parted the press, and said, "He will not wake;
This is the endless sleep, and we must make
A bed deep down for him beneath the sod;
For know, my sons, there is a mighty God
Angry with all man's race, but most with me.
I fled from out His land in vain!—'tis He
Who came and slew the lad; for He has found
This home of ours, and we shall all be bound
By the harsh bands of His most cruel will,
Which any moment may some dear one kill.

Nay, though we live for countless moons, at last
We and all ours shall die like summers past.
This is Jehovah's will, and He is strong;
I thought the way I travelled was too long
For Him to follow me: my thought was vain!
He walks unseen, but leaves a track of pain,
Pale Death His footprint is, and He will come again!"

And a new spirit from that hour came o'er
The race of Cain: soft idlesse was no more,
But even the sunshine had a heart of care,
Smiling with hidden dread — a mother fair
Who folding to her breast a dying child
Beams with feigned joy that but makes sadness mild.
Death was now lord of Life, and at his word
Time, vague as air before, new terrors stirred,
With measured wing now audibly arose
Throbbing through all things to some unknown close.
Now glad Content by clutching Haste was torn,
And Work grew eager, and Device was born.

It seemed the light was never loved before,
Now each man said, "'Twill go and come no more."
No budding branch, no pebble from the brook,
No form, no shadow, but new dearness took
From the one thought that life must have an end;
And the last parting now began to send
Diffusive dread through love and wedded bliss,
Thrilling them into finer tenderness.
Then Memory disclosed her face divine,
That like the calm nocturnal lights doth shine
Within the soul, and shows the sacred graves,
And shows the presence that no sunlight craves,
No space, no warmth, but moves among them all;
Gone and yet here, and coming at each call,
With ready voice and eyes that understand,
And lips that ask a kiss, and dear responsive hand.

Thus to Cain's race death was tear-watered seed
Of various life and action-shaping need.
But chief the sons of Lamech felt the stings
Of new ambition, and the force that springs

In passion beating on the shores of fate.
They said, "There comes a night when all too late
The mind shall long to prompt the achieving hand,
The eager thought behind closed portals stand,
And the last wishes to the mute lips press
Buried ere death in silent helplessness.
Then while the soul its way with sound can cleave,
And while the arm is strong to strike and heave,
Let soul and arm give shape that will abide
And rule above our graves, and power divide
With that great god of day, whose rays must bend
As we shall make the moving shadows tend.
Come, let us fashion acts that are to be,
When we shall lie in darkness silently,
As our young brother doth, whom yet we see
Fallen and slain, but reigning in our will
By that one image of him pale and still."

For Lamech's sons were heroes of their race:
Jabal, the eldest, bore upon his face
The look of that calm river-god, the Nile,
Mildly secure in power that needs not guile.

But Tubal-Cain was restless as the fire
That glows and spreads and leaps from high to higher
Where'er is aught to seize or to subdue;
Strong as a storm he lifted or o'erthrew,
His urgent limbs like granite bowlders grew,
Such bowlders as the plunging torrent wears
And roaring rolls around through countless years.
But strength that still on movement must be fed,
Inspiring thought of change, devices bred,
And urged his mind through earth and air to rove
For force that he could conquer if he strove,
For lurking forms that might new tasks fulfil
And yield unwilling to his stronger will.
Such Tubal-Cain. But Jubal had a frame
Fashioned to finer senses, which became
A yearning for some hidden soul of things,
Some outward touch complete on inner springs
That vaguely moving bred a lonely pain,
A want that did but stronger grow with gain
Of all good else, as spirits might be sad
For lack of speech to tell us they are glad.

Now Jabal learned to tame the lowing kine,
And from their udders drew the snow-white wine
That stirs the innocent joy, and makes the stream
Of elemental life with fulness teem;
The star-browed calves he nursed with feeding hand,
And sheltered them, till all the little band
Stood mustered gazing at the sunset way
Whence he would come with store at close of day.
He soothed the silly sheep with friendly tone,
And reared their staggering lambs, that, older grown,
Followed his steps with sense-taught memory;
Till he, their shepherd, could their leader be,
And guide them through the pastures as he would,
With sway that grew from ministry of good.
He spread his tents upon the grassy plain
Which, eastward widening like the open main,
Showed the first whiteness 'neath the morning star;
Near him his sister, deft, as women are,
Plied her quick skill in sequence to his thought
Till the hid treasures of the milk she caught
Revealed like pollen 'mid the petals white,
The golden pollen, virgin to the light.

Even the she-wolf with young, on rapine bent,
He caught and tethered in his mat-walled tent,
And cherished all her little sharp-nosed young
Till the small race with hope and terror clung
About his footsteps, till each new-reared brood,
Remoter from the memories of the wood,
More glad discerned their common home with man.
This was the work of Jabal: he began
The pastoral life, and, sire of joys to be,
Spread the sweet ties that bind the family
O'er dear dumb souls that thrilled at man's caress,
And shared his pain with patient helpfulness.

But Tubal-Cain had caught and yoked the fire,
Yoked it with stones that bent the flaming spire
And made it roar in prisoned servitude
Within the furnace, till with force subdued
It changed all forms he willed to work upon,
Till hard from soft, and soft from hard, he won.
The pliant clay he moulded as he would,
And laughed with joy when 'mid the heat it stood

Shaped as his hand had chosen, while the mass
That from his hold, dark, obstinate, would pass,
He drew all glowing from the busy heat,
All breathing as with life that he could beat
With thundering hammer, making it obey
His will creative, like the pale soft clay.
Each day he wrought and better than he planned,
Shape breeding shape beneath his restless hand.
(The soul without still helps the soul within,
And its deft magic ends what we begin.)
Nay, in his dreams his hammer he would wield
And seem to see a myriad types revealed,
Then spring with wondering triumphant cry,
And, lest the inspiring vision should go by,
Would rush to labor with that plastic zeal
Which all the passion of our life can steal
For force to work with. Each day saw the birth
Of various forms, which, flung upon the earth,
Seemed harmless toys to cheat the exacting hour,
But were as seeds instinct with hidden power.
The axe, the club, the spikèd wheel, the chain,
Held silently the shrieks and moans of pain;

And near them latent lay in share and spade,
In the strong bar, the saw, and deep-curved blade,
Glad voices of the hearth and harvest-home,
The social good, and all earth's joy to come.
Thus to mixed ends wrought Tubal; and they say,
Some things he made have lasted to this day;
As, thirty silver pieces that were found
By Noah's children buried in the ground.
He made them from mere hunger of device,
Those small white discs; but they became the price
The traitor Judas sold his Master for;
And men still handling them in peace and war
Catch foul disease, that comes as appetite,
And lurks and clings as withering, damning blight.
But Tubal-Cain wot not of treachery,
Nor greedy lust, nor any ill to be,
Save the one ill of sinking into nought,
Banished from action and act-shaping thought.
He was the sire of swift-transforming skill,
Which arms for conquest man's ambitious will;
And round him gladly, as his hammer rung,
Gathered the elders and the growing young:

These handled vaguely, and those plied the tools,
Till, happy chance begetting conscious rules,
The home of Cain with industry was rife,
And glimpses of a strong persistent life,
Panting through generations as one breath,
And filling with its soul the blank of death.

Jubal, too, watched the hammer, till his eyes,
No longer following its fall or rise,
Seemed glad with something that they could not see,
But only listened to — some melody,
Wherein dumb longings inward speech had found,
Won from the common store of struggling sound.
Then, as the metal shapes more various grew,
And, hurled upon each other, resonance drew,
Each gave new tones, the revelations dim
Of some external soul that spoke for him:
The hollow vessel's clang, the clash, the boom,
Like light that makes wide spiritual room
And skyey spaces in the spaceless thought,
To Jubal such enlargèd passion brought,
That love, hope, rage, and all experiènce,
Were fused in vaster being, fetching thence

Concords and discords, cadences and cries
That seemed from some world-shrouded soul to rise,
Some rapture more intense, some mightier rage,
Some living sea that burst the bounds of man's brief age.

Then with such blissful trouble and glad care
For growth within unborn as mothers bear,
To the far woods he wandered, listening,
And heard the birds their little stories sing
In notes whose rise and fall seem melted speech —
Melted with tears, smiles, glances — that can reach
More quickly through our frame's deep-winding night,
And without thought raise thought's best fruit, delight.
Pondering, he sought his home again and heard
The fluctuant changes of the spoken word:
The deep remonstrance and the argued want,
Insistent first in close monotonous chant,
Next leaping upward to defiant stand
Or downward beating like the resolute hand;

The mother's call, the children's answering cry,
The laugh's light cataract tumbling from on high;
The suasive repetitions Jabal taught,
That timid browsing cattle homeward brought:
The clear-winged fugue of echoes vanishing;
And through them all the hammer's rhythmic ring.
Jubal sat lonely, all around was dim,
Yet his face glowed with light revealed to him:
For as the delicate stream of odor wakes
The thought-wed sentience, and some image makes
From out the mingled fragments of the past,
Finely compact in wholeness that will last,
So streamed as from the body of each sound
Subtler pulsations, swift as warmth, which found
All prisoned germs and all their powers unbound,
Till thought self-luminous flamed from memory,
And in creative vision wandered free.
Then Jubal, standing, rapturous arms upraised,
And on the dark with eager eyes he gazed,
As had some manifested god been there.
It was his thought he saw: the presence fair

Of unachieved achievement, the high task,
The mighty unborn spirit that doth ask
With irresistible cry for blood and breath,
Till feeding its great life we sink in death.

He said, "Were now those mighty tones and cries
That from the giant soul of earth arise,
Those groans of some great travail heard from far,
Some power at wrestle with the things that are,
Those sounds which vary with the varying form
Of clay and metal, and in sightless swarm
Fill the wide space with tremors: were these wed
To human voices with such passion fed
As does but glimmer in our common speech,
But might flame out in tones whose changing reach
Surpassing meagre need, informs the sense
With fuller union, finer difference —
Were this great vision, now obscurely bright
As morning hills that melt in new-poured light,
Wrought into solid form and living sound,
Moving with ordered throb and sure rebound,

Then — Nay, I Jubal will that work begin!
The generations of our race shall win
New life, that grows from out the heart of this,
As spring from winter, or as lovers' bliss
From out the dull unknown of unwaked energies."

Thus he resolved, and in the soul-fed light
Of coming ages waited through the night,
Watching for that near dawn whose chiller ray
Showed but the unchanged world of yesterday;
Where all the order of his dream divine
Lay like Olympian forms within the mine;
Where fervor that could fill the earthly round
With thongèd joys of form-begotten sound
Must shrink intense within the patient power
That lonely labors through the niggard hour.
Such patience have the heroes who begin,
Sailing the first toward lands which others win.
Jubal must dare as great beginners dare,
Strike form's first way in matter rude and bare,
And, yearning vaguely toward the plenteous choir
Of the world's harvest, make one poor small lyre.

He made it, and from out its measured frame
Drew the harmonic soul, whose answers came
With guidance sweet and lessons of delight
Teaching to ear and hand the blissful Right,
Where strictest law is gladness to the sense,
And all desire bends toward obedience.
Then Jubal poured his triumph in a song—
The rapturous word that rapturous notes prolong
As radiance streams from smallest things that
 burn,
Or thought of loving into love doth turn.
And still his lyre gave companionship
In sense-taught concert as of lip with lip.
Alone amid the hills at first he tried
His wingèd song; then with adoring pride
And bridegroom's joy at leading forth his bride,
He said, "This wonder which my soul hath found,
This heart of music in the might of sound,
Shall forthwith be the share of all our race,
And like the morning gladden common space:
The song shall spread and swell as rivers do,
And I will teach our youth with skill to woo

This living lyre, to know its secret will,
Its fine division of the good and ill.
So shall men call me sire of harmony,
And where great Song is, there my life shall be."
Thus glorying as a god beneficent,
Forth from his solitary joy he went
To bless mankind. It was at evening,
When shadows lengthen from each westward thing,
When imminence of change makes sense more fine,
And light seems holier in its grand decline.
The fruit-trees wore their studded coronal,
Earth and her children were at festival,
Glowing as with one heart and one consent —
Thought, love, trees, rocks, in sweet warm radiance
blent.

The tribe of Cain was resting on the ground,
The various ages wreathed in one broad round.
Here lay, while children peeped o'er his huge thighs,
The sinewy man imbrowned by centuries;
Here the broad-bosomed mother of the strong
Looked, like Demeter, placid o'er the throng

Of young lithe forms whose rest was movement too —
Tricks, prattle, nods, and laughs that lightly flew,
And swayings as of flower-beds where Love blew.
For all had feasted well upon the flesh
Of juicy fruits, on nuts, and honey fresh,
And now their wine was health-bred merriment,
Which through the generations circling went,
Leaving none sad, for even father Cain
Smiled as a Titan might, despising pain.
Jabal sat circled with a playful ring
Of children, lambs and whelps, whose gambolling,
With tiny hoofs, paws, hands, and dimpled feet,
Made barks, bleats, laughs, in pretty hubbub meet.
But Tubal's hammer rang from far away,
Tubal alone would keep no holiday,
His furnace must not slack for any feast,
For of all hardship, work he counted least;
He scorned all rest but sleep, where every dream
Made his repose more potent action seem.

Yet with health's nectar some strange thirst was blent,
The fateful growth, the unnamed discontent,

The inward shaping toward some unborn power,
Some deeper-breathing act, the being's flower.
After all gestures, words, and speech of eyes,
The soul had more to tell, and broke in sighs.
Then from the east, with glory on his head
Such as low-slanting beams on corn-waves spread,
Came Jubal with his lyre: there 'mid the throng,
Where the blank space was, poured a solemn song,
Touching his lyre to full harmonic throb
And measured pulse, with cadences that sob,
Exult and cry, and search the inmost deep
Where the dark sources of new passion sleep.
Joy took the air, and took each breathing soul,
Embracing them in one entrancèd whole,
Yet thrilled each varying frame to various ends,
As Spring new-waking through the creature sends
Or rage or tenderness; more plenteous life
Here breeding dread, and there a fiercer strife.
He who had lived through twice three centuries,
Whose months monotonous, like trees on trees
In hoary forests, stretched a backward maze,
Dreamed himself dimly through the travelled days

Till in clear light he paused, and felt the sun
That warmed him when he was a little one;
Knew that true heaven, the recovered past,
The dear small Known amid the Unknown vast,
And in that heaven wept. But younger limbs
Thrilled toward the future, that bright land which swims
In western glory, isles and streams and bays,
Where hidden pleasures float in golden haze.
And in all these the rhythmic influence,
Sweetly o'ercharging the delighted sense,
Flowed out in movements, little waves that spread
Enlarging, till in tidal union led
The youths and maidens both alike long-tressed,
By grace-inspiring melody possessed,
Rose in slow dance, with beauteous floating swerve
Of limbs and hair, and many a melting curve
Of ringèd feet swayed by each close-linked palm:
Then Jubal poured more rapture in his psalm,
The dance fired music, music fired the dance,
The glow diffusive lit each countenance,
Till all the circling tribe arose and stood
With glad yet awful shock of that mysterious good.

Even Tubal caught the sound, and wondering came,
Urging his sooty bulk like smoke-wrapt flame
Till he could see his brother with the lyre,
The work for which he lent his furnace-fire
And diligent hammer, witting nought of this —
This power in metal shape which made strange bliss,
Entering within him like a dream full-fraught
With new creations finished in a thought.

The sun had sunk, but music still was there,
And when this ceased, still triumph filled the air:
It seemed the stars were shining with delight
And that no night was ever like this night.
All clung with praise to Jubal: some besought
That he would teach them his new skill; some caught,
Swiftly as smiles are caught in looks that meet,
The tone's melodic change and rhythmic beat:
'Twas easy following where invention trod —
All eyes can see when light flows out from God.

And thus did Jubal to his race reveal
Music their larger soul, where woe and weal

Filling the resonant chords, the song, the dance,
Moved with a wider-wingèd utterance.
Now many a lyre was fashioned, many a song
Raised echoes new, old echoes to prolong,
Till things of Jubal's making were so rife,
"Hearing myself," he said, "hems in my life,
And I will get me to some far-off land,
Where higher mountains under heaven stand
And touch the blue at rising of the stars,
Whose song they hear where no rough mingling mars
The great clear voices. Such lands there must be,
Where varying forms make varying symphony —
Where other thunders roll amid the hills,
Some mightier wind a mightier forest fills
With other strains through other-shapen boughs;
Where bees and birds and beasts that hunt or browse
Will teach me songs I know not. Listening there,
My life shall grow like trees both tall and fair
That rise and spread and bloom toward fuller fruit each year."

He took a raft, and travelled with the stream
Southward for many a league, till he might deem
He saw at last the pillars of the sky,
Beholding mountains whose white majesty
Rushed through him as new awe, and made new song
That swept with fuller wave the chords along,
Weighting his voice with deep religious chime,
The iteration of slow chant sublime.

It was the region long inhabited
By all the race of Seth; and Jubal said,
"Here have I found my thirsty soul's desire,
Eastward the hills touch heaven, and evening's fire
Flames through deep waters; I will take my rest,
And feed anew from my great mother's breast,
The sky-clasped Earth, whose voices nurture me
As the flowers' sweetness doth the honey-bee."
He lingered wandering for many an age,
And, sowing music, made high heritage
For generations far beyond the Flood —
For the poor late-begotten human brood
Born to life's weary brevity and perilous good.

And ever as he travelled he would climb
The farthest mountain, yet the heavenly chime,
The mighty tolling of the far-off spheres
Beating their pathway, never touched his ears.
But wheresoe'er he rose, the heavens rose,
And the far-gazing mountain could disclose
Nought but a wider earth; until one height
Showed him the ocean stretched in liquid light,
And he could hear its multitudinous roar,
Its plunge and hiss upon the pebbled shore:
Then Jubal silent sat, and touched his lyre no more.

He thought, "The world is great, but I am weak,
And where the sky bends is no solid peak
To give me footing, but instead, this main
Like myriad maddened horses thundering o'er the plain.

"New voices come to me where'er I roam,
My heart too widens with its widening home:
But song grows weaker, and the heart must break
For lack of voice, or fingers that can wake

The lyre's full answer; nay, its chords were all
Too few to meet the growing spirit's call.
The former songs seem little, yet no more
Can soul, hand, voice, with interchanging lore
Tell what the earth is saying unto me:
The secret is too great, I hear confusedly.

"No farther will I travel: once again
My brethren I will see, and that fair plain
Where I and song were born. There fresh-voiced youth
Will pour my strains with all the early truth
Which now abides not in my voice and hands,
But only in the soul, the will that stands
Helpless to move. My tribe remembering
Will cry, ''Tis he!' and run to greet me, welcoming."

The way was weary. Many a date-palm grew,
And shook out clustered gold against the blue,
While Jubal, guided by the steadfast spheres,
Sought the dear home of those first eager years,

When, with fresh vision fed, the fuller will
Took living outward shape in pliant skill;
For still he hoped to find the former things,
And the warm gladness recognition brings.
His footsteps erred among the mazy woods
And long illusive sameness of the floods,
Winding and wandering. Through far regions, strange
With Gentile homes and faces, did he range,
And left his music in their memory,
And left at last, when nought besides would free
His homeward steps from clinging hands and cries,
The ancient lyre. And now in ignorant eyes
No sign remained of Jubal, Lamech's son,
That mortal frame wherein was first begun
The immortal life of song. His withered brow
Pressed over eyes that held no lightning now,
His locks streamed whiteness on the hurrying air,
The unresting soul had worn itself quite bare
Of beauteous token, as the outworn might
Of oaks slow dying, gaunt in summer's light.

His full deep voice toward thinnest treble ran:
He was the rune-writ story of a man.
And so at last he neared the well-known land,
Could see the hills in ancient order stand
With friendly faces whose familiar gaze
Looked through the sunshine of his childish days;
Knew the deep-shadowed folds of hanging woods,
And seemed to see the selfsame insect broods
Whirling and quivering o'er the flowers — to hear
The selfsame cuckoo making distance near.
Yea, the dear Earth, with mother's constancy,
Met and embraced him, and said, "Thou art he!
This was thy cradle, here my breast was thine,
Where feeding, thou didst all thy life intwine
With my sky-wedded life in heritage divine."

But wending ever through the watered plain,
Firm not to rest save in the home of Cain,
He saw dread Change, with dubious face and cold
That never kept a welcome for the old,
Like some strange heir upon the hearth, arise
Saying, "This home is mine." He thought his eyes

Mocked all deep memories, as things new made,
Usurping sense, make old things shrink and fade
And seem ashamed to meet the staring day.
His memory saw a small foot-trodden way,
His eyes a broad far-stretching paven road
Bordered with many a tomb and fair abode;
The little city that once nestled low
As buzzing groups about some central glow,
Spread like a murmuring crowd o'er plain and
steep,
Or monster huge in heavy-breathing sleep.
His heart grew faint, and tremblingly he sank
Close by the wayside on a weed-grown bank,
Not far from where a new-raised temple stood,
Sky-roofed, and fragrant with wrought cedar-wood.
The morning sun was high; his rays fell hot
On this hap-chosen, dusty, common spot,
On the dry withered grass and withered man:
That wondrous frame where melody began
Lay as a tomb defaced that no eye cared to scan.
But while he sank far music reached his ear.
He listened until wonder silenced fear,

And gladness wonder; for the broadening stream
Of sound advancing was his early dream,
Brought like fulfilment of forgotten prayer;
As if his soul, breathed out upon the air,
Had held the invisible seeds of harmony
Quick with the various strains of life to be.
He listened: the sweet mingled difference
With charm alternate took the meeting sense;
Then bursting like some shield-broad lily red,
Sudden and near the trumpet's notes out-spread,
And soon his eyes could see the metal flower,
Shining upturned, out on the morning pour
Its incense audible; could see a train
From out the street slow-winding on the plain
With lyres and cymbals, flutes and psalteries,
While men, youths, maids, in concert sang to these
With various throat, or in succession poured,
Or in full volume mingled. But one word
Ruled each recurrent rise and answering fall,
As when the multitudes adoring call
On some great name divine, their common soul,
The common need, love, joy, that knits them in one
whole.

The word was "Jubal!" . . . "Jubal" filled the
air,
And seemed to ride aloft, a spirit there,
Creator of the choir, the full-fraught strain
That grateful rolled itself to him again.
The aged man adust upon the bank —
Whom no eye saw — at first with rapture drank
The bliss of music, then, with swelling heart,
Felt, this was his own being's greater part,
The universal joy once born in him.
But when the train, with living face and limb
And vocal breath, came nearer and more near,
The longing grew that they should hold him dear;
Him, Lamech's son, whom all their fathers knew,
The breathing Jubal — him, to whom their love was
due.
All was forgotten but the burning need
To claim his fuller self, to claim the deed
That lived away from him, and grew apart,
While he as from a tomb, with lonely heart,
Warmed by no meeting glance, no hand that pressed,
Lay chill amid the life his life had blessed.

What though his song should spread from man's
small race
Out through the myriad worlds that people space,
And make the heavens one joy-diffusing choir?—
Still 'mid that vast would throb the keen desire
Of this poor aged flesh, this eventide,
This twilight soon in darkness to subside,
This little pulse of self, that, having glowed
Through thrice three centuries, and divinely strewed
The light of music through the vague of sound,
Ached smallness still in good that had no bound.

For no eye saw him, while with loving pride
Each voice with each in praise of Jubal vied.
Must he in conscious trance, dumb, helpless lie
While all that ardent kindred passed him by?
His flesh cried out to live with living men,
And join that soul which to the inward ken
Of all the hymning train was present there.
Strong passion's daring sees not aught to dare:
The frost-locked starkness of his frame low-bent,
His voice's penury of tones long spent,

He felt not; all his being leaped in flame
To meet his kindred as they onward came
Slackening and wheeling toward the temple's face:
He rushed before them to the glittering space,
And, with a strength that was but strong desire,
Cried, "I am Jubal, I! . . . I made the lyre!"

The tones amid a lake of silence fell
Broken and strained, as if a feeble bell
Had tuneless pealed the triumph of a land
To listening crowds in expectation spanned.
Sudden came showers of laughter on that lake;
They spread along the train from front to wake
In one great storm of merriment, while he
Shrank doubting whether he could Jubal be,
And not a dream of Jubal, whose rich vein
Of passionate music came with that dream-pain,
Wherein the sense slips off from each loved thing,
And all appearance is mere vanishing.
But ere the laughter died from out the rear,
Anger in front saw profanation near;

Jubal was but a name in each man's faith
For glorious power untouched by that slow death
Which creeps with creeping time ; this too, the spot,
And this the day, it must be crime to blot,
Even with scoffing at a madman's lie :
Jubal was not a name to wed with mockery.

Two rushed upon him : two, the most devout
In honor of great Jubal, thrust him out,
And beat him with their flutes. 'Twas little need ;
He strove not, cried not, but with tottering speed,
As if the scorn and howls were driving wind
That urged his body, serving so the mind
Which could but shrink and yearn, he sought the
screen
Of thorny thickets, and there fell unseen.
The immortal name of Jubal filled the sky,
While Jubal lonely laid him down to die.
He said within his soul, " This is the end :
O'er all the earth to where the heavens bend
And hem men's travel, I have breathed my soul :
I lie here now the remnant of that whole,

The embers of a life, a lonely pain;
As far-off rivers to my thirst were vain,
So of my mighty years nought comes to me
again.

"Is the day sinking? Softest coolness springs
From something round me: dewy shadowy wings
Enclose me all around — no, not above —
Is moonlight there? I see a face of love,
Fair as sweet music when my heart was strong:
Yea — art thou come again to me, great Song?"

The face bent over him like silver night
In long-remembered summers; that calm light
Of days which shine in firmaments of thought,
That past unchangeable, from change still wrought.
And there were tones that with the vision blent:
He knew not if that gaze the music sent,
Or music that calm gaze: to hear, to see,
Was but one undivided ecstasy:
The raptured senses melted into one,
And parting life a moment's freedom won

From in and outer, as a little child
Sits on a bank and sees blue heavens mild
Down in the water, and forgets its limbs,
And knoweth nought save the blue heaven that swims.
"Jubal," the face said, "I am thy loved Past,
The soul that makes thee one from first to last.
I am the angel of thy life and death,
Thy outbreathed being drawing its last breath.
Am I not thine alone, a dear dead bride
Who blest thy lot above all men's beside?
Thy bride whom thou wouldst never change, nor take
Any bride living, for that dead one's sake?
Was I not all thy yearning and delight,
Thy chosen search, thy senses' beauteous Right,
Which still had been the hunger of thy frame
In central heaven, hadst thou been still the same?
Wouldst thou have asked aught else from any god —
Whether with gleaming feet on earth he trod
Or thundered through the skies — aught else for share
Of mortal good, than in thy soul to bear

The growth of song, and feel the sweet unrest
Of the world's spring-tide in thy conscious breast?
No, thou hadst grasped thy lot with all its pain,
Nor loosed it any painless lot to gain
Where music's voice was silent; for thy fate
Was human music's self incorporate:
Thy senses' keenness and thy passionate strife
Were flesh of *her* flesh and her womb of life.
And greatly hast thou lived, for not alone
With hidden raptures were her secrets shown,
Buried within thee, as the purple light
Of gems may sleep in solitary night;
But thy expanding joy was still to give,
And with the generous air in song to live
Feeding the wave of ever-widening bliss
Where fellowship means equal perfectness.
And on the mountains in thy wandering
Thy feet were beautiful as blossomed spring,
That turns the leafless wood to love's glad home,
For with thy coming Melody was come.
This was thy lot, to feel, create, bestow,
And that immeasurable life to know

From which the fleshly self falls shrivelled, dead,
A seed primeval that has forests bred.
It is the glory of the heritage
Thy life has left, that makes thy outcast age:
Thy limbs shall lie dark, tombless on this sod,
Because thou shinest in man's soul, a god,
Who found and gave new passion and new joy
That nought but Earth's destruction can destroy.
Thy gifts to give was thine of men alone:
'Twas but in giving that thou couldst atone
For too much wealth amid their poverty."—

The words seemed melting into symphony,
The wings upbore him, and the gazing song
Was floating him the heavenly space along,
Where mighty harmonies all gently fell
Through veiling vastness, like the far-off bell,
Till, ever onward through the choral blue,
He heard more faintly and more faintly knew,
Quitting mortality, a quenched sun-wave,
The All-creating Presence for his grave.

1869.

AGATHA.

AGATHA.

Come with me to the mountain, not where rocks
Soar harsh above the troops of hurrying pines,
But where the earth spreads soft and rounded breasts
To feed her children; where the generous hills
Lift a green isle betwixt the sky and plain
To keep some Old World things aloof from change.
Here too 'tis hill and hollow: new-born streams
With sweet enforcement, joyously compelled
Like laughing children, hurry down the steeps,
And make a dimpled chase athwart the stones;
Pine-woods are black upon the heights, the slopes
Are green with pasture, and the bearded corn
Fringes the blue above the sudden ridge:
A little world whose round horizon cuts

This isle of hills with heaven for a sea,
Save in clear moments when southwestward gleams
France by the Rhine, melting anon to haze.
The monks of old chose here their still retreat,
And called it by the Blessed Virgin's name,
Sancta Maria, which the peasant's tongue,
Speaking from out the parent's heart that turns
All loved things into little things, has made
Sanct Märgen, — Holy little Mary, dear
As all the sweet home things she smiles upon,
The children and the cows, the apple-trees,
The cart, the plough, all named with that caress
Which feigns them little, easy to be held,
Familiar to the eyes and hand and heart.
What though a Queen? She puts her crown away
And with her little Boy wears common clothes,
Caring for common wants, remembering
That day when good Saint Joseph left his work
To marry her with humble trust sublime.

The monks are gone, their shadows fall no more
Tall-frocked and cowled athwart the evening fields

At milking time; their silent corridors
Are turned to homes of bare-armed, aproned men,
Who toil for wife and children. But the bells,
Pealing on high from two quaint convent towers,
Still ring the Catholic signals, summoning
To grave remembrance of the larger life
That bears our own, like perishable fruit
Upon its heaven-wide branches. At their sound
The shepherd-boy far off upon the hill,
The workers with the saw and at the forge,
The triple generation round the hearth, —
Grandames and mothers and the flute-voiced girls, —
Fall on their knees, and send forth prayerful cries
To the kind Mother with the little Boy,
Who pleads for helpless men against the storm,
Lightning and plagues and all terrific shapes
Of power supreme.
Within the prettiest hollow of these hills,
Just as you enter it, upon the slope
Stands a low cottage neighbored cheerily
By running water, which, at farthest end
Of the same hollow, turns a heavy mill,

And feeds the pasture for the miller's cows,
Blanchi and Nägeli, Veilchen and the rest,
Matrons with faces as Griselda mild,
Coming at call. And on the farthest height
A little tower looks out above the pines,
Where mounting you will find a sanctuary
Open and still; without, the silent crowd
Of heaven-planted, incense-mingling flowers;
Within, the altar where the Mother sits
'Mid votive tablets hung from far-off years
By peasants succored in the peril of fire,
Fever, or flood, who thought that Mary's love,
Willing but not omnipotent, had stood
Between their lives and that dread power which slew
Their neighbor at their side. The chapel bell
Will melt to gentlest music ere it reach
That cottage on the slope, whose garden-gate
Has caught the rose-tree boughs, and stands ajar;
So does the door, to let the sunbeams in;
For in the slanting sunbeams angels come
And visit Agatha who dwells within, —
Old Agatha, whose cousins Kate and Nell

Are housed by her in Love and Duty's name,
They being feeble, with small withered wits,
And she believing that the higher gift
Was given to be shared. So Agatha
Shares her one room, all neat on afternoons,
As if some memory were sacred there
And every thing within the four low walls
An honored relic.
One long summer's day
An angel entered at the rose-hung gate,
With skirts pale blue, a brow to quench the pearl,
Hair soft and blonde as infants', plenteous
As hers who made the wavy lengths once speak
The grateful worship of a rescued soul.
The angel paused before the open door
To give good-day. "Come in," said Agatha.
I followed close, and watched and listened there.
The angel was a lady, noble, young,
Taught in all seemliness that fits a court,
All lore that shapes the mind to delicate use,
Yet quiet, lowly, as a meek white dove
That with its presence teaches gentleness.

Men called her Countess Linda ; little girls
In Freiburg town, orphans whom she caressed,
Said Mamma Linda : yet her years were few,
Her outward beauties all in budding-time,
Her virtues the aroma of the plant
That dwells in all its being, root, stem, leaf,
And waits not ripeness.
"Sit," said Agatha.
Her cousins were at work in neighboring homes,
But yet she was not lonely ; all things round
Seemed filled with noiseless yet responsive life,
As of a child at breast that gently clings :
Not sunlight only or the breathing flowers
Or the swift shadows of the birds and bees,
But all the household goods, which, polished fair
By hands that cherished them for service done,
Shone as with glad content. The wooden beams
Dark and yet friendly, easy to be reached,
Bore three white crosses for a speaking sign ;
The walls had little pictures hung a-row,
Telling the stories of Saint Ursula,
And Saint Elizabeth, the lowly queen ;

And on the bench that served for table too,
Skirting the wall to save the narrow space,
There lay the Catholic books, inherited
From those old times when printing still was young
With stout-limbed promise, like a sturdy boy.
And in the farthest corner stood the bed
Where o'er the pillow hung two pictures wreathed
With fresh-plucked ivy: one the Virgin's death,
And one her flowering tomb, while high above
She smiling bends, and lets her girdle down
For ladder to the soul that cannot trust
In life which outlasts burial. Agatha
Sat at her knitting, aged, upright, slim,
And spoke her welcome with mild dignity.
She kept the company of kings and queens
And mitred saints who sat below the feet
Of Francis with the ragged frock and wounds;
And Rank for her meant Duty, various,
Yet equal in its worth, done worthily.
Command was service; humblest service done
By willing and discerning souls was glory.
Fair Countess Linda sat upon the bench,

Close fronting the old knitter, and they talked
With sweet antiphony of young and old.

AGATHA.

You like our valley, lady? I am glad
You thought it well to come again. But rest—
The walk is long from Master Michael's inn.

COUNTESS LINDA.

Yes, but no walk is prettier.

AGATHA.

It is true:
There lacks no blessing here, the waters all
Have virtues like the garments of the Lord,
And heal much sickness; then, the crops and cows
Flourish past speaking, and the garden flowers,
Pink, blue, and purple, 'tis a joy to see
How they yield honey for the singing bees.
I would the whole world were as good a home.

COUNTESS LINDA.

And you are well off, Agatha? — your friends
Left you a certain bread: is it not so?

AGATHA.

Not so at all, dear lady. I had nought,
Was a poor orphan; but I came to tend
Here in this house, an old afflicted pair,
Who wore out slowly; and the last who died,
Full thirty years ago, left me this roof
And all the household stuff. It was great wealth;
And so I had a home for Kate and Nell.

COUNTESS LINDA.

But how, then, have you earned your daily bread
These thirty years?

AGATHA.

Oh, that is easy earning.
We help the neighbors, and our bit and sup

Is never failing: they have work for us
In house and field, all sorts of odds and ends,
Patching and mending, turning o'er the hay,
Holding sick children, — there is always work;
And they are very good, — the neighbors are:
Weigh not our bits of work with weight and scale,
But glad themselves with giving us good shares
Of meat and drink; and in the big farm-house
When cloth comes home from weaving, the good wife
Cuts me a piece, — this very gown, — and says,
"Here, Agatha, you old maid, you have time
To pray for Hans who is gone soldiering:
The saints might help him, and they have much to do,
'Twere well they were besought to think of him."
She spoke half jesting, but I pray, I pray
For poor young Hans. I take it much to heart
That other people are worse off than I, —
I ease my soul with praying for them all.

COUNTESS LINDA.

That is your way of singing, Agatha;

Just as the nightingales pour forth sad songs,
And when they reach men's ears they make men's
hearts
Feel the more kindly.

AGATHA.

Nay, I cannot sing:
My voice is hoarse, and oft I think my prayers
Are foolish, feeble things; for Christ is good
Whether I pray or not, — the Virgin's heart
Is kinder far than mine; and then I stop
And feel I can do nought towards helping men,
Till out it comes, like tears that will not hold,
And I must pray again for all the world.
'Tis good to me, — I mean the neighbors are:
To Kate and Nell too. I have money saved
To go on pilgrimage the second time.

COUNTESS LINDA.

And do you mean to go on pilgrimage
With all your years to carry, Agatha?

AGATHA.

The years are light, dear lady: 'tis my sins
Are heavier than I would. And I shall go
All the way to Einsiedeln with that load:
I need to work it off.

COUNTESS LINDA.

What sort of sins,
Dear Agatha? I think they must be small.

AGATHA.

Nay, but they may be greater than I know;
'Tis but dim light I see by. So I try
All ways I know of to be cleansed and pure:
I would not sink where evil spirits are.
There's perfect goodness somewhere: so I strive.

COUNTESS LINDA.

You were the better for that pilgrimage
You made before? The shrine is beautiful;
And then you saw fresh country all the way.

AGATHA.

Yes, that is true. And ever since that time
The world seems greater, and the Holy Church
More wonderful. The blessed pictures all,
The heavenly images with books and wings,
Are company to me through the day and night.
The time! the time! It never seemed far back,
Only to father's father and his kin
That lived before him. But the time stretched out
After that pilgrimage: I seemed to see
Far back, and yet I knew time lay behind,
As there are countries lying still behind
The highest mountains, there in Switzerland
Oh, it is great to go on pilgrimage!

COUNTESS LINDA.

Perhaps some neighbors will be pilgrims too,
And you can start together in a band.

AGATHA.

Not from these hills: people are busy here,

The beasts want tendance. One who is not missed
Can go and pray for others who must work.
I owe it to all neighbors, young and old;
For they are good past thinking, — lads and girls
Given to mischief, merry naughtiness,
Quiet it, as the hedgehogs smooth their spines,
For fear of hurting poor old Agatha.
'Tis pretty: why, the cherubs in the sky
Look young and merry, and the angels play
On citherns, lutes, and all sweet instruments.
I would have young things merry. See the Lord!
A little baby playing with the birds;
And how the Blessed Mother smiles at him.

COUNTESS LINDA.

I think you are too happy, Agatha,
To care for heaven. Earth contents you well.

AGATHA.

Nay, nay, I shall be called, and I shall go
Right willingly. I shall get helpless, blind,

Be like an old stalk to be plucked away:
The garden must be cleared for young spring plants.
'Tis home beyond the grave, the most are there,
All those we pray to, all the Church's lights, —
And poor old souls are welcome in their rags:
One sees it by the pictures. Good Saint Ann,
The Virgin's mother, she is very old,
And had her troubles with her husband too.
Poor Kate and Nell are younger far than I,
But they will have this roof to cover them.
I shall go willingly; and willingness
Makes the yoke easy and the burden light.

COUNTESS LINDA.

When you go southward in your prilgrimage,
Come to see me in Freiburg, Agatha.
Where you have friends you should not go to inns.

AGATHA.

Yes, I will gladly come to see you, lady.
And you will give me sweet hay for a bed,

And in the morning I shall wake betimes
And start when all the birds begin to sing.

COUNTESS LINDA.

You wear your smart clothes on the pilgrimage,
Such pretty clothes as all the women here
Keep by them for their best: a velvet cap
And collar golden-broidered? They look well
On old and young alike.

AGATHA.

Nay, I have none, —
Never had better clothes than these you see.
Good clothes are pretty, but one sees them best
When others wear them, and I somehow thought
'Twas not worth while. I had so many things
More than some neighbors, I was partly shy
Of wearing better clothes than they, and now
I am so old and custom is so strong
'Twould hurt me sore to put on finery.

COUNTESS LINDA.

Your gray hair is a crown, dear Agatha.
Shake hands; good-by. The sun is going down,
And I must see the glory from the hill.

I staid among those hills; and oft heard more
Of Agatha. I liked to hear her name,
As that of one half grandame and half saint,
Uttered with reverent playfulness. The lads
And younger men all called her mother, aunt,
Or granny, with their pet diminutives,
And bade their lasses and their brides behave
Right well to one who surely made a link
'Twixt faulty folk and God by loving both:
Not one but counted service done by her,
Asking no pay save just her daily bread.
At feasts and weddings, when they passed in groups
Along the vale, and the good country wine,
Being vocal in them, made them choir along
In quaintly mingled mirth and piety,
They fain must jest and play some friendly trick

On three old maids; but when the moment came
Always they bated breath, and made their sport,
Gentle as feather-stroke, that Agatha
Might like the waking for the love it showed.
Their song made happy music 'mid the hills,
For nature tuned their race to harmony,
And poet Hans, the tailor, wrote them songs
That grew from out their life, as crocuses
From out the meadow's moistness. 'Twas his song
They oft sang, wending homeward from a feast, —
The song I give you. It brings in, you see,
Their gentle jesting with the three old maids.

Midnight by the chapel bell!
Homeward, homeward all, farewell!
I with you, and you with me,
Miles are short with company.
Heart of Mary, bless the way,
Keep us all by night and day!

Moon and stars at feast with night
Now have drunk their fill of light.

Home they hurry, making time
Trot apace, like merry rhyme.
Heart of Mary, mystic rose,
Send us all a sweet repose!

Swiftly through the wood down hill,
Run till you can hear the mill.
Toni's ghost is wandering now,
Shaped just like a snow-white cow.
Heart of Mary, morning star,
Ward off danger, near or far!

Toni's wagon with its load
Fell and crushed him in the road
'Twixt these pine-trees. Never fear!
Give a neighbor's ghost good cheer.
Holy Babe, our God and Brother,
Bind us fast to one another!

Hark! the mill is at its work,
Now we pass beyond the murk

To the hollow, where the moon
Makes her silvery afternoon.
Good Saint Joseph, faithful spouse,
Help us all to keep our vows!

Here the three old maidens dwell,
Agatha and Kate and Nell;
See, the moon shines on the thatch,
We will go and shake the latch.
Heart of Mary, cup of joy,
Give us mirth without alloy!

Hush, 'tis here, no noise, sing low,
Rap with gentle knuckles — so!
Like the little tapping birds,
On the door; then sing good words.
Meek Saint Anna, old and fair,
Hallow all the snow-white hair!

Little maidens old, sweet dreams!
Sleep one sleep till morning beams.

Mothers ye, who help us all,
Quick at hand, if ill befall.
Holy Gabriel, lily-laden,
Bless the aged mother-maiden!

Forward, mount the broad hillside
Swift as soldiers when they ride.
See the two towers how they peep,
Round-capped giants, o'er the steep.
Heart of Mary, by thy sorrow,
Keep us upright through the morrow!

Now they rise quite suddenly
Like a man from bended knee,
Now Saint Märgen is in sight,
Here the roads branch off — good-night!
Heart of Mary, by thy grace,
Give us with the saints a place!

1868.

ARMGART.

ARMGART.

SCENE I.

A Salon lit with lamps, and ornamented with green plants. An open piano, with many scattered sheets of music. Bronze busts of Beethoven and Gluck on pillars opposite each other. A small table spread with supper. To FRÄULEIN WALPURGA, *who advances with a slight lameness of gait from an adjoining room, enters* GRAF DORNBERG *at the opposite door in a travelling dress.*

GRAF.

Good-morning, Fräulein!

WALPURGA.

What, so soon returned?
I feared your mission kept you still at Prague.

GRAF.

But now arrived! You see my travelling dress.
I hurried from the panting, roaring steam
Like any courier of embassy
Who hides the fiends of war within his bag.

WALPURGA.

You know that Armgart sings to-night?

GRAF.

Has sung!
'Tis close on half-past nine. The *Orpheus*
Lasts not so long. Her spirits — were they high?
Was Leo confident?

WALPURGA.

He only feared
Some tameness at beginning. Let the house
Once ring, he said, with plaudits, she is safe.

GRAF.

And Armgart?

WALPURGA.

She was stiller than her wont.
But once, at some such trivial word of mine,
As that the highest prize might yet be won
By her who took the second — she was roused.
"For me," she said, "I triumph or I fail.
I never strove for any second prize."

GRAF.

Poor human-hearted singing-bird! She bears
Cæsar's ambition in her delicate breast,
And nought to still it with but quivering song!

WALPURGA.

I had not for the world been there to-night:
Unreasonable dread oft chills me more
Than any reasonable hope can warm.

GRAF.

You have a rare affection for your cousin;
As tender as a sister's.

WALPURGA.

Nay, I fear
My love is little more than what I felt
For happy stories when I was a child.
She fills my life that would be empty else,
And lifts my nought to value by her side.

GRAF.

She is reason good enough, or seems to be,
Why all were born whose being ministers
To her completeness. Is it most her voice
Subdues us? or her instinct exquisite,
Informing each old strain with some new grace,
Which takes our sense like any natural good?
Or most her spiritual energy,
That sweeps us in the current of her song?

WALPURGA.

I know not. Losing either, we should lose
That whole we call our Armgart. For herself,

She often wonders what her life had been
Without that voice for channel to her soul.
She says, it must have leaped through all her
    limbs —
Made her a Mænad — made her snatch a brand,
And fire some forest, that her rage might mount
In crashing roaring flames through half a land,
Leaving her still and patient for a while.
"Poor wretch!" she says, of any murderess —
"The world was cruel, and she could not sing:
I carry my revenges in my throat;
I love in singing, and am loved again."

GRAF.

Mere mood! I cannot yet believe it more.
Too much ambition has unwomaned her;
But only for a while. Her nature hides
One half its treasures by its very wealth,
Taxing the hours to show it.

WALPURGA.

Hark! she comes.

Enter LEO *with a wreath in his hand, holding the door open for* ARMGART, *who wears a furred mantle and hood. She is followed by her maid, carrying an armful of bouquets.*

LEO.

Place for the queen of song!

GRAF (*advancing towards* ARMGART, *who throws off her hood and mantle, and shows a star of brilliants in her hair*).

A triumph, then.
You will not be a niggard of your joy,
And chide the eagerness that came to share it.

ARMGART.

O kind! you hastened your return for me.
I would you had been there to hear me sing!
Walpurga, kiss me: never tremble more
Lest Armgart's wing should fail her. She has found

This night the region where her rapture breathes —
Pouring her passion on the air made live
With human heart-throbs. Tell them, Leo, tell
them
How I outsang your hope, and made you cry
Because Gluck could not hear me. That was folly!
He sang, not listened: every linkèd note
Was his immortal pulse that stirred in mine,
And all my gladness is but part of him.
Give me the wreath.
[*She crowns the bust of* GLUCK.

LEO (*sardonically*).

Ay, ay, but mark you this:
It was not part of him — that trill you made
In spite of me and reason!

ARMGART.

You were wrong —
Dear Leo, you were wrong: the house was held
As if a storm were listening with delight,
And hushed its thunder.

LEO.

Will you ask the house
To teach you singing? Quit your *Orpheus* then,
And sing in farces grown to operas,
Where all the prurience of the full-fed mob
Is tickled with melodic impudence:
Jerk forth burlesque bravuras, square your arms
Akimbo with a tavern wench's grace,
And set the splendid compass of your voice
To lyric jigs. Go to! I thought you meant
To be an artist — lift your audience
To see your vision, not trick forth a show
To please the grossest taste of grossest numbers.

ARMGART (*taking up* LEO'S *hand, and kissing it*).

Pardon, good Leo, I am penitent.
I will do penance: sing a hundred trills
Into a deep-dug grave, then burying them
As one did Midas' secret, rid myself
Of naughty exultation. Oh I trilled
At nature's prompting, like the nightingales.
Go scold them, dearest Leo.

LEO.

I stop my ears.
Nature in Gluck inspiring Orpheus,
Has done with nightingales. Are bird-beaks lips?

GRAF.

Truce to rebukes! Tell us — who were not there —
The double drama: how the expectant house
Took the first notes.

WALPURGA (*turning from her occupation of decking the room with the flowers*).

Yes, tell us all, dear Armgart.
Did you feel tremors? Leo, how did she look?
Was there a cheer to greet her?

LEO.

Not a sound.
She walked like Orpheus in his solitude,
And seemed to see nought but what no man saw.

'Twas famous. Not the Schroeder-Devrient
Had done it better. But your blessed public
Had never any judgment in cold blood —
Thinks all perhaps were better otherwise,
Till rapture brings a reason.

ARMGART (*scornfully*).

I knew that!
The women whispered, "Not a pretty face!"
The men, "Well, well, a goodly length of limb:
She bears the chiton." — It were all the same
Were I the Virgin Mother, and my stage
The opening heavens at the Judgment-day:
Gossips would peep, jog elbows, rate the price
Of such a woman in the social mart.
What were the drama of the world to them,
Unless they felt the hell-prong?

LEO.

Peace, now, peace!
I hate my phrases to be smothered o'er
With sauce of paraphrase, my sober tune

Made bass to rambling trebles, showering down
In endless demi-semi-quavers.

ARMGART (*taking a bon-bon from the table, uplifting it before putting it into her mouth, and turning away*).

Mum!

GRAF.

Yes, tell us all the glory, leave the blame.

WALPURGA.

You first, dear Leo — what you saw and heard;
Then Armgart — she must tell us what she felt.

LEO.

Well! The first notes came clearly, firmly forth.
And I was easy, for behind those rills
I knew there was a fountain. I could see
The house was breathing gently, heads were still;
Parrot opinion was struck meekly mute,
And human hearts were swelling. Armgart stood

As if she had been new-created there,
And found her voice which found a melody.
The minx! Gluck had not written, nor I taught:
Orpheus was Armgart, Armgart Orpheus.
Well, well, all through the *scena* I could feel
The silence tremble now, now poise itself
With added weight of feeling, till at last
Delight o'er-toppled it. The final note
Had happy drowning in the unloosed roar
That surged and ebbed and ever surged again,
Till expectation kept it pent awhile
Ere Orpheus returned. Pfui! He was changed:
My demi-god was pale, had downcast eyes
That quivered like a bride's who fain would send
Backward the rising tear.

ARMGART (*advancing, but then turning away, as if to check her speech*).

I *was* a bride,
As nuns are at their spousals.

LEO.

Ay, my lady,

That moment will not come again: applause
May come and plenty; but the first, first draught!
[*Snaps his fingers.*
Music has sounds for it — I know no words.
I felt it once myself when they performed
My overture to Sintram. Well! 'tis strange,
We know not pain from pleasure in such joy.

ARMGART (*turning quickly*).

Oh, pleasure has cramped dwelling in our souls,
And when full Being comes must call on pain
To lend it liberal space.

WALPURGA.

I hope the house
Kept a reserve of plaudits: I am jealous
Lest they had dulled themselves for coming good
That should have seemed the better and the best.

LEO.

No, 'twas a revel where they had but quaffed
Their opening cup. I thank the artist's star,

His audience keeps not sober: once afire,
They flame towards climax, though his merit hold
But fairly even.

ARMGART (*her hand on* LEO'S *arm*).

Now, now, confess the truth:
I sang still better to the very end —
All save the trill; I give that up to you,
To bite and growl at. Why, you said yourself,
Each time I sang, it seemed new doors were open
That you might hear heaven clearer.

LEO (*shaking his finger*).

I was raving.

ARMGART.

I am not glad with that mean vanity
Which knows no good beyond its appetite
Full feasting upon praise! I am only glad,
Being praised for what I know is worth the praise;
Glad of the proof that I myself have part

In what I worship! At the last applause —
Seeming a roar of tropic winds that tossed
The handkerchiefs and many-colored flowers,
Falling like shattered rainbows all around —
Think you I felt myself a *prima donna?*
No, but a happy spiritual star
Such as old Dante saw, wrought in a rose
Of light in Paradise, whose only self
Was consciousness of glory wide-diffused,
Music, life, power — I moving in the midst
With a sublime necessity of good.

LEO (*with a shrug*).

I thought it was a *prima donna* came
Within the side-scenes; ay, and she was proud
To find the bouquet from the royal box
Enclosed a jewel-case, and proud to wear
A star of brilliants, quite an earthly star,
Valued by thalers. Come, my lady, own
Ambition has five senses, and a self
That gives it good warm lodging when it sinks
Plump down from ecstasy.

ARMGART.

Own it? why not?
Am I a sage whose words must fall like seed
Silently buried toward a far-off spring?
I sing to living men, and my effect
Is like the summer's sun, that ripens corn
Or now or never. If the world brings me gifts,
Gold, incense, myrrh — 'twill be the needful sign
That I have stirred it as the high year stirs
Before I sink to winter.

GRAF.

Ecstasies
Are short — most happily! We should but lose
Were Armgart borne too commonly and long
Out of the self that charms us. Could I choose,
She were less apt to soar beyond the reach
Of woman's foibles, innocent vanities,
Fondness for trifles like that pretty star
Twinkling beside her cloud of ebon hair.

ARMGART (*taking out the gem, and looking at it*).

This little star! I would it were the seed
Of a whole Milky Way, if such bright shimmer
Were the sole speech men told their rapture with
At Armgart's music. Shall I turn aside
From splendors which flash out the glow I make,
And live to make, in all the chosen breasts
Of half a Continent? No, may it come,
That splendor! May the day be near when men
Think much to let my horses draw me home,
And new lands welcome me upon their beach,
Loving me for my fame. That is the truth
Of what I wish, nay, yearn for. Shall I lie?
Pretend to seek obscurity — to sing
In hope of disregard? A vile pretence!
And blasphemy besides. For what is fame
But the benignant strength of One, transformed
To joy of Many? Tributes, plaudits come
As necessary breathing of such joy;
And may they come to me!

GRAF.

The auguries
Point clearly that way. Is it no offence
To wish the eagle's wing may find repose,
As feebler wings do, in a quiet nest?
Or has the taste of fame already turned
The Woman to a Muse . . .

LEO (*going to the table*).

Who needs no supper.
I am her priest, ready to eat her share
Of good Walpurga's offerings.

WALPURGA.

Armgart, come.
Graf, will you come?

GRAF.

Thanks, I play truant here,
And must retrieve my self-indulged delay.

But will the Muse receive a votary
At any hour to-morrow?

ARMGART.

Any hour
After rehearsal, after twelve at noon.

SCENE II.

The same Salon, morning. ARMGART *seated, in her bonnet and walking-dress. The* GRAF *standing near her against the piano.*

GRAF.

Armgart, to many minds the first success
Is reason for desisting. I have known
A man so versatile, he tried all arts,
But when in each by turns he had achieved
Just so much mastery as made men say,

"He could be king here if he would," he threw
The lauded skill aside. He hates, said one,
The level of achieved pre-eminence,
He must be conquering still; but others said—

ARMGART.

The truth, I hope: he had a meagre soul,
Holding no depth where love could root itself.
"Could if he would?" True greatness ever wills—
It lives in wholeness if it live at all,
And all its strength is knit with constancy.

GRAF.

He used to say himself he was too sane
To give his life away for excellence
Which yet must stand, an ivory statuette
Wrought to perfection through long lonely years,
Huddled in the mart of mediocrities.
He said, the very finest doing wins
The admiring only; but to leave undone,
Promise and not fulfil, like buried youth,

Wins all the envious, makes them sigh your name
As that fair Absent, blameless Possible,
Which could alone impassion them; and thus,
Serene negation has free gift of all,
Panting achievement struggles, is denied,
Or wins to lose again. What say you, Armgart?
Truth has rough flavors if we bite it through;
I think this sarcasm came from out its core
Of bitter irony.

ARMGART.

It is the truth
Mean souls select to feed upon. What then?
Their meanness is a truth, which I will spurn.
The praise I seek lives not in envious breath,
Using my name to blight another's deed.
I sing for love of song and that renown
Which is the spreading act, the world-wide share,
Of good that I was born with. Had I failed —
Well, that had been a truth most pitiable.
I cannot bear to think what life would be
With high hope shrunk to endurance, stunted aims

Like broken lances ground to eating-knives,
A self sunk down to look with level eyes
At low achievemennt, doomed from day to day
To distaste of its consciousness. But I —

GRAF.

Have won, not lost, in your decisive throw.
And I too glory in this issue ; yet
The public verdict has no potency
To sway my judgment of what Armgart is :
My pure delight in her would be but sullied,
If it o'erflowed with mixture of men's praise.
And had she failed, I should have said, " The pearl
Remains a pearl for me, reflects the light
With the same fitness that first charmed my gaze —
Is worth as fine a setting now as then."

ARMGART (*rising*).

Oh you are good ! But why will you rehearse
The talk of cynics, who with insect eyes
Explore the secrets of the rubbish-heap ?
I hate your epigrams and pointed saws

Whose narrow truth is but broad falsity.
Confess your friend was shallow.

GRAF.

I confess
Life is not rounded in an epigram,
And saying aught, we leave a world unsaid.
I quoted, merely to shape forth my thought
That high success has terrors when achieved —
Like preternatural spouses whose dire love
Hangs perilous on slight observances:
Whence it were possible that Armgart crowned
Might turn and listen to a pleading voice,
Though Armgart striving in the race was deaf.
You said you dared not think what life had been
Without the stamp of eminence; have you thought
How you will bear the poise of eminence
With dread of sliding? Paint the future out
As an unchecked and glorious career,
'Twill grow more strenuous by the very love
You bear to excellence, the very fate
Of human powers, which tread at every step
On possible verges.

ARMGART.

I accept the peril.
I choose to walk high with sublimer dread
Rather than crawl in safety. And, besides,
I am an artist as you are a noble:
I ought to bear the burthen of my rank.

GRAF.

Such parallels, dear Armgart, are but snares
To catch the mind with seeming argument —
Small baits of likeness 'mid disparity.
Men rise the higher as their task is high,
The task being well achieved. A woman's rank
Lies in the fulness of her womanhood:
Therein alone she is royal.

ARMGART.

Yes, I know
The oft-taught Gospel: "Woman, thy desire
Shall be that all superlatives on earth
Belong to men, save the one highest kind —

To be a mother. Thou shalt not desire
To do aught best save pure subservience:
Nature has willed it so!" O blessed Nature!
Let her be arbitress; she gave me voice
Such as she only gives a woman child,
Best of its kind, gave me ambition too,
That sense transcendent which can taste the joy
Of swaying multitudes, of being adored
For such achievement, needed excellence,
As man's best art must wait for, or be dumb.
Men did not say, when I had sung last night,
"'Twas good, nay, wonderful, considering
She is a woman" — and then turn to add,
"Tenor or baritone had sung her songs
Better, of course: she's but a woman spoiled."
I beg your pardon, Graf, you said it.

GRAF.

No!
How should I say it, Armgart? I who own
The magic of your nature-given art
As sweetest effluence of your womanhood,

Which, being to my choice the best, must find
The best of utterance. But this I say:
Your fervid youth beguiles you; you mistake
A strain of lyric passion for a life
Which in the spending is a chronicle
With ugly pages. Trust me, Armgart, trust me;
Ambition exquisite as yours which soars
Toward something quintessential you call fame,
Is not robust enough for this gross world
Whose fame is dense with false and foolish breath.
Ardor, a-twin with nice refining thought,
Prepares a double pain. Pain had been saved,
Nay, purer glory reached, had you been throned
As woman only, holding all your art
As attribute to that dear sovereignty —
Concentring your power in home delights
Which penetrate and purify the world.

ARMGART.

What, leave the opera with my part ill-sung
While I was warbling in a drawing-room?
Sing in the chimney-corner to inspire

My husband reading news? Let the world hear
My music only in his morning speech
Less stammering than most honorable men's?
No! tell me that my song is poor, my art
The piteous feat of weakness aping strength—
That were fit proem to your argument.
Till then, I am an artist by my birth—
By the same warrant that I am a woman:
Nay, in the added rarer gift I see
Supreme vocation: if a conflict comes,
Perish—no, not the woman, but the joys
Which men make narrow by their narrowness.
Oh I am happy! The great masters write
For women's voices, and great Music wants me!
I need not crush myself within a mould
Of theory called Nature: I have room
To breathe and grow unstunted.

GRAF.

Armgart, hear me.
I meant not that our talk should hurry on
To such collision. Foresight of the ills

Thick shadowing your path, drew on my speech
Beyond intention. True, I came to ask
A great renunciation, but not this
Towards which my words at first perversely strayed,
As if in memory of their earlier suit,
Forgetful . . . .
Armgart, do you remember too? the suit
Had but postponement, was not quite disdained —
Was told to wait and learn — what it has learned —
A more submissive speech.

ARMGART (*with some agitation*).

Then it forgot
Its lesson cruelly. As I remember,
'Twas not to speak save to the artist crowned,
Nor speak to her of casting off her crown.

GRAF.

Nor will it, Armgart. I come not to seek
Any renunciation save the wife's,
Which turns away from other possible love

Future and worthier to take his love
Who asks the name of husband. He who sought
Armgart obscure, and heard her answer, "Wait"—
May come without suspicion now to seek
Armgart applauded.

ARMGART (*turning towards him*).

Yes, without suspicion
Of aught save what consists with faithfulness
In all expressed intent. Forgive me, Graf—
I am ungrateful to no soul that loves me—
To you most grateful. Yet the best intent
Grasps but a living present which may grow
Like any unfledged bird. You are a noble,
And have a high career; just now you said
'Twas higher far than aught a woman seeks
Beyond mere womanhood. You claim to be
More than a husband, but could not rejoice
That I were more than wife. What follows, then?
You choosing me with such persistency
As is but stretched-out rashness, soon must find
Our marriage asks concessions, asks resolve

To share renunciation or demand it.
Either we both renounce a mutual ease,
As in a nation's need both man and wife
Do public services, or one of us
Must yield that something else for which each lives
Besides the other. Men are reasoners:
That premise of superior claims perforce
Urges conclusion — "Armgart, it is you."

GRAF.

But if I say I have considered this
With strict prevision, counted all the cost
Which that great good of loving you demands —
Questioned my stores of patience, half-resolved
To live resigned without a bliss whose threat
Touched you as well as me — and finally,
With impetus of undivided will
Returned to say, "You shall be free as now;
Only accept the refuge, shelter, guard,
My love will give your freedom" — then your words
Are hard accusal.

ARMGART.

Well, I accuse myself.
My love would be accomplice of your will.

GRAF.

Again — my will?

ARMGART.

Oh, your unspoken will.
Your silent tolerance would torture me,
And on that rack I should deny the good
I yet believed in.

GRAF.

Then I am the man
Whom you would love?

ARMGART.

Whom I refuse to love!
No, I will live alone, and pour my pain
With passion into music, where it turns

To what is best within my better self.
I will not take for husband one who deems
The thing my soul acknowledges as good —
The thing I hold worth striving, suffering for,
To be a thing dispensed with easily,
Or else the idol of a mind infirm.

GRAF.

Armgart, you are ungenerous; you strain
My thought beyond its mark. Our difference
Lies not so deep as love — as union
Through a mysterious fitness that transcends
Formal agreement.

ARMGART.

It lies deep enough
To chafe the union. If many a man
Refrains, degraded, from the utmost right,
Because the pleadings of his wife's small fears
Are little serpents biting at his heel,—
How shall a woman keep her steadfastness

Beneath a frost within her husband's eyes
Where coldness scorches? Graf, it is your sorrow
That you love Armgart. Nay, it is her sorrow
That she may not love you.

GRAF.

Woman, it seems,
Has enviable power to love or not
According to her will.

ARMGART.

She has the will—
I have — who am one woman — not to take
Disloyal pledges that divide her will.
The man who marries me must wed my Art —
Honor and cherish it, not tolerate.

GRAF.

The man is yet to come whose theory
Will weigh as nought with you against his love.

ARMGART.

Whose theory will plead beside his love.

GRAF.

Himself a singer, then? who knows no life
Out of the opera books, where tenor parts
Are found to suit him?

ARMGART.

You are bitter, Graf.
Forgive me; seek the woman you deserve,
All grace, all goodness, who has not yet found
A meaning in her life, nor any end
Beyond fulfilling yours. The type abounds.

GRAF.

And happily, for the world.

ARMGART.

Yes, happily.

Let it excuse me that my kind is rare:
Commonness is its own security.

GRAF.

Armgart, I would with all my soul I knew
The man so rare that he could make your life
As woman sweet to you, as artist safe.

ARMGART.

Oh I can live unmated, but not live
Without the bliss of singing to the world,
And feeling all my world respond to me.

GRAF.

May it be lasting. Then, we two must part?

ARMGART.

I thank you from my heart for all. Farewell!

SCENE III.—A YEAR LATER.

The same Salon. WALPURGA *is standing looking towards the window with an air of uneasiness.* DOCTOR GRAHN.

DOCTOR.

Where is my patient, Fräulein?

WALPURGA.

Fled! escaped!
Gone to rehearsal. Is it dangerous?

DOCTOR.

No, no; her throat is cured. I only came
To hear her try her voice. Had she yet sung?

WALPURGA.

No: she had meant to wait for you. She said,
"The Doctor has a right to my first song."
Her gratitude was full of little plans,

But all were swept away like gathered flowers
By sudden storm. She saw this opera bill—
It was a wasp to sting her: she turned pale,
Snatched up her hat and mufflers, said in haste,
"I go to Leo—to rehearsal—none
Shall sing Fidelio to-night but me!"
Then rushed down stairs.

DOCTOR (*looking at his watch*).

And this, not long ago?

WALPURGA.

Barely an hour.

DOCTOR.

I will come again
Returning from Charlottenburg at one.

WALPURGA.

Doctor, I feel a strange presentiment.
Are you quite easy?

DOCTOR.

She can take no harm.
'Twas time for her to sing: her throat is well.
It was a fierce attack, and dangerous;
I had to use strong remedies, but — well!
At one, dear Fräulein, we shall meet again.

SCENE IV. — TWO HOURS LATER.

WALPURGA *starts up, looking towards the door.* ARMGART *enters, followed by* LEO. *She throws herself on a chair which stands with its back towards the door, speechless, not seeming to see any thing.* WALPURGA *casts a questioning, terrified look at* LEO. *He shrugs his shoulders, and lifts up his hands behind* ARMGART, *who sits like a helpless image, while* WALPURGA *takes off her hat and mantle.*

WALPURGA.

Armgart, dear Armgart (*kneeling, and taking her hands*), only speak to me,
Your poor Walpurga. Oh your hands are cold!
Clasp mine, and warm them! I will kiss them warm.

(ARMGART *looks at her an instant, then draws away her hands, and, turning aside, buries her face against the back of the chair,* WALPURGA *rising, and standing near.*)

(DOCTOR GRAHN *enters.*)

DOCTOR.

News! stirring news to-day! wonders come thick.

ARMGART (*starting up at the first sound of his voice, and speaking vehemently*).

Yes, thick, thick, thick! and you have murdered it!
Murdered my voice — poisoned the soul in me,
And kept me living.
You never told me that your cruel cures
Were clogging films — a mouldy, dead'ning blight —

A lava-mud to crust and bury me,
Yet hold me living in a deep, deep tomb,
Crying unheard forever! Oh your cures
Are devils' triumphs: you can rob, maim, slay,
And keep a hell on the other side your cure
Where you can see your victim quivering
Between the teeth of torture — see a soul
Made keen by loss — all anguish with a good
Once known and gone! (*Turns and sinks back on her chair.*)
O misery, misery!
You might have killed me, might have let me sleep
After my happy day, and wake — not here!
In some new unremembered world, — not here,
Where all is faded, flat — a feast broke off —
Banners all meaningless — exulting words
Dull, dull — a drum that lingers in the air
Beating to melody which no man hears.

DOCTOR (*after a moment's silence.*)

A sudden check has shaken you, poor child!
All things seem livid, tottering to your sense,

From inward tumult. Stricken by a threat
You see your terrors only. Tell me, Leo:
'Tis not such utter loss. (LEO, *with a shrug, goes quietly out.*)
The freshest bloom
Merely, has left the fruit; the fruit itself . . .

ARMGART.

Is ruined, withered, is a thing to hide
Away from scorn or pity. Oh you stand
And look compassionate now, but when Death came
With mercy in his hands, you hindered him.
I did not choose to live and have your pity.
You never told me, never gave me choice
To die a singer, lightning-struck, unmaimed,
Or live what you would make me with your cures —
A self accursed with consciousness of change,
A mind that lives in nought but members lopped,
A power turned to pain — as meaningless
As letters fallen asunder that once made
A hymn of rapture. Oh, I had meaning once,

Like day and sweetest air. What am I now?
The millionth woman in superfluous herds.
Why should I be, do, think? 'Tis thistle-seed,
That grows and grows to feed the rubbish-heap.
Leave me alone!

DOCTOR.

Well, I will come again;
Send for me when you will, though but to rate me.
That is medicinal — a letting blood.

ARMGART.

Oh there is one physician, only one,
Who cures and never spoils. Him I shall send for;
He comes readily.

DOCTOR (*to* WALPURGA).

One word, dear Fräulein.

SCENE V.

ARMGART, WALPURGA.

ARMGART.

Walpurga, have you walked this morning?

WALPURGA.

No.

ARMGART.

Go, then, and walk; I wish to be alone.

WALPURGA.

I will not leave you.

ARMGART.

Will not, at my wish?

WALPURGA.

Will not, because you wish it. Say no more,
But take this draught.

ARMGART.

The Doctor gave it you ?
It is an anodyne. Put it away.
He cured me of my voice, and now he wants
To cure me of my vision and resolve —
Drug me to sleep that I may wake again
Without a purpose, abject as the rest
To bear the yoke of life. He shall not cheat me
Of that fresh strength which anguish gives the soul,
The inspiration of revolt, ere rage
Slackens to faltering. Now I see the truth.

WALPURGA (*setting down the glass*).

Then you must see a future in your reach,
With happiness enough to make a dower
For two of modest claims.

ARMGART.

Oh you intone
That chant of consolation wherewith ease
Makes itself easier in the sight of pain.

WALPURGA.

No; I would not console you, but rebuke.

ARMGART.

That is more bearable. Forgive me, dear.
Say what you will. But now I want to write.
(*She rises, and moves towards a table*).

WALPURGA.

I say then, you are simply fevered, mad;
You cry aloud at horrors that would vanish
If you would change the light, throw into shade
The loss you aggrandize, and let day fall
On good remaining, nay on good refused
Which may be gain now. Did you not reject
A woman's lot more brilliant, as some held,
Than any singer's? It may still be yours.
Graf Dornberg loved you well.

ARMGART.

Not me, not me.

He loved one well who was like me in all
Save in a voice which made that All unlike
As diamond is to charcoal. Oh, a man's love!
Think you he loves a woman's inner self
Aching with loss of loveliness? — as mothers
Cleave to the palpitating pain that dwells
Within their misformed offspring?

WALPURGA.

But the Graf
Chose you as simple Armgart — had preferred
That you should never seek for any fame
But such as matrons have who rear great sons.
And therefore you rejected him; but now —

ARMGART.

Ay, now — now he would see me as I am,
(*she takes up a hand-mirror*),
Russet and songless as a missel-thrush.
An ordinary girl — a plain brown girl,
Who, if some meaning flash from out her words,

Shocks as a disproportioned thing — a Will
That, like an arm astretch and broken off,
Has nought to hurl — the torso of a soul.
I sang him into love of me: my song
Was consecration, lifted me apart
From the crowd chiselled like me, sister forms,
But empty of divineness. Nay, my charm
Was half that I could win fame, yet renounce!
A wife with glory possible absorbed
Into her husband's actual.

WALPURGA.

For shame!
Armgart, you slander him. What would you say
If now he came to you and asked again
That you would be his wife?

ARMGART.

No, and thrice no!
It would be pitying constancy, not love,
That brought him to me now. I will not be
A pensioner in marriage. Sacraments

Are not to feed the paupers of the world.
If he were generous — I am generous too.

WALPURGA.

Proud, Armgart, but not generous.

ARMGART.

Say no more.
He will not know until —

WALPURGA.

He knows already.

ARMGART (*quickly*).

Is he come back?

WALPURGA.

Yes, and will soon be here.
The Doctor had twice seen him, and would go
From hence again to see him.

ARMGART.

Well, he knows.

It is all one.

WALPURGA.

What if he were outside?

I hear a footstep in the ante-room.

ARMGART (*raising herself, and assuming calmness*).

Why let him come, of course. I shall behave
Like what I am, a common personage
Who looks for nothing but civility.
I shall not play the fallen heroine,
Assume a tragic part, and throw out cues
For a beseeching lover.

WALPURGA.

Some one raps.

(*Goes to the door.*)

A letter — from the Graf.

ARMGART.

Then open it.

(WALPURGA *still offers it.*)

Nay, my head swims. Read it. I cannot see.

(WALPURGA *opens it, reads and pauses.*)

Read it. Have done! No matter what it is.

WALPURGA (*reads in a low, hesitating voice*).

"I am deeply moved — my heart is rent, to hear of your illness and its cruel result, just now communicated to me by Dr. Grahn. But surely it is possible that this result may not be permanent. For youth such as yours, Time may hold in store something more than resignation: who shall say that it does not hold renewal? I have not dared to ask admission to you in the hours of a recent shock, but I cannot depart on a long mission without tendering my sympathy and my farewell. I start this evening for the Caucasus, and thence I proceed to India, where I am intrusted by the Government with business which may be of long duration."

(WALPURGA *sits down dejectedly.*)

ARMGART (*after a slight shudder, bitterly*).

The Graf has much discretion. I am glad.
He spares us both a pain, not seeing me.
What I like least is that consoling hope —
That empty cup, so neatly ciphered "Time,"
Handed me as a cordial for despair.
(*Slowly and dreamily*) Time — what a word to fling as charity!
Bland neutral word for slow, dull-beating pain —
Days, months, and years! — If I would wait for them!

(*She takes up her hat and puts it on, then wraps her mantle round her.* WALPURGA *leaves the room.*)

Why, this is but beginning. (WALP. *re-enters.*)
Kiss me, dear.
I am going now — alone — out — för a walk.
Say you will never wound me any more
With such cajolery as nurses use
To patients amorous of a crippled life.
Flatter the blind: I see.

WALPURGA.

Well, I was wrong.
In haste to soothe, I snatched at flickers merely.
Believe me, I will flatter you no more.

ARMGART.

Bear witness, I am calm. I read my lot
As soberly as if it were a tale
Writ by a creeping feuilletonist, and called
"The Woman's Lot: a Tale of Everyday:"
A middling woman's, to impress the world
With high superfluousness; her thoughts a crop
Of chick-weed errors or of pot-herb facts,
Smiled at like some child's drawing on a slate.
"Genteel?" "Oh yes, gives lessons; not so good
As any man's would be, but cheaper far."
"Pretty?" "No: yet she makes a figure fit
For good society. Poor thing, she sews
Both late and early, turns and alters all
To suit the changing mode. Some widower

Might do well, marrying her; but in these
days! . . .
Well, she can somewhat eke her narrow gains
By writing, just to furnish her with gloves
And droskies in the rain. They print her things
Often for charity." — Oh a dog's life!
A harnessed dog's, that draws a little cart
Voted a nuisance! I am going now.

WALPURGA.

Not now, the door is locked.

ARMGART.

Give me the key!

WALPURGA.

Locked on the outside. Gretchen has the key:
She is gone on errands.

ARMGART.

What, you dare to keep me
Your prisoner?

WALPURGA.

And have I not been yours?
Your wish has been a bolt to keep me in.
Perhaps that middling woman whom you paint
With far-off scorn . . .

ARMGART.

I paint what I must be!
What is my soul to me without the voice
That gave its freedom?—gave it one grand touch
And made it nobly human?—Prisoned now,
Prisoned in all the petty mimicries
Called woman's knowledge, that will fit the world
As doll-clothes fit a man. I can do nought
Better than what a million women do—
Must drudge among the crowd, and feel my life
Beating upon the world without response,
Beating with passion through an insect's horn
That moves a millet-seed laboriously.
If I *would* do it!

WALPURGA (*coldly*).

And why should you not?

ARMGART (*turning quickly*).

Because Heaven made me royal — wrought me out
With subtle finish towards pre-eminence,
Made every channel of my soul converge
To one high function, and then flung me down,
That breaking I might turn to subtlest pain.
An inborn passion gives a rebel's right;
I would rebel and die in twenty worlds
Sooner than bear the yoke of thwarted life,
Each keenest sense turned into keen distaste,
Hnnger not satisfied but kept alive
Breathing in languor half a century.
All the world now is but a rack of threads
To twist and dwarf me into pettiness
And basely feigned content, the placid mask
Of woman's misery.

WALPURGA (*indignantly*).

Ay, such a mask
As the few born like you to easy joy,
Cradled in privilege, take for natural
On all the lowly faces that must look
Upward to you! What revelation now
Shows you the mask or gives presentiment
Of sadness hidden? You who every day
These five years saw me limp to wait on you,
And thought the order perfect which gave *me*,
The girl without pretension to be aught,
A splendid cousin for my happiness:
To watch the night through when her brain was fired
With too much gladness — listen, always listen
To what *she* felt, who having power had right
To feel exorbitantly, and submerge
The souls around her with the poured-out flood
Of what must be ere she were satisfied!
That was feigned patience, was it? Why not love,
Love nurtured even with that strength of self
Which found no room save in another's life?

Oh such as I know joy by negatives,
And all their deepest passion is a pang
Till they accept their pauper's heritage,
And meekly live from out the general store
Of joy they were born stripped of. I accept —
Nay, now would sooner choose it than the wealth
Of natures you call royal, who can live
In mere mock knowledge of their fellows' woe,
Thinking their smiles may heal it.

ARMGART (*tremulously*)

Nay, Walpurga,
I did not make a palace of my joy
To shut the world's truth from me. All my good
Was that I touched the world, and made a part
In the world's dower of beauty, strength, and bliss;
It was the glimpse of consciousness divine
Which pours out day, and sees the day is good.
Now I am fallen dark; I sit in gloom,
Remembering bitterly. Yet you speak truth;
I wearied you, it seems; took all your help
As cushioned nobles use a weary serf,
Not looking at his face.

WALPURGA.

Oh, I but stand
As a small symbol for a mighty sum —
The sum of claims unpaid for myriad lives;
I think you never set your loss beside
That mighty deficit. Is your work gone —
The prouder queenly work that paid itself,
And yet was overpaid with men's applause?
Are you no longer chartered, privileged,
But sunk to simple woman's penury,
To ruthless Nature's chary average —
Where is the rebel's right for you alone?
Noble rebellion lifts a common load;
But what is he who flings his own load off,
And leaves his fellows toiling? Rebel's right?
Say rather, the deserter's. Oh, you smiled
From your clear height on all the million lots
Which yet you brand as abject.

ARMGART.

I was blind

With too much happiness: true vision comes
Only, it seems, with sorrow. Were there one
This moment near me, suffering what I feel,
And needing me for comfort in her pang —
Then it were worth the while to live; not else.

WALPURGA.

One — near you — why, they throng! you hardly stir
But your act touches them. We touch afar.
For did not swarthy slaves of yesterday
Leap in their bondage at the Hebrews' flight,
Which touched them through the thrice millennial
dark?
But you can find the sufferer you need
With touch less subtle.

ARMGART.

Who has need of me?

WALPURGA.

Love finds the need it fills. But you are hard.

ARMGART.

Is it not you, Walpurga, who are hard?
You humored all my wishes till to-day,
When fate has blighted me

WALPURGA.

You would not hear
The "chant of consolation:" words of hope
Only imbittered you. Then hear the truth —
A lame girl's truth, whom no one ever praised
For being cheerful. "It is well," they said:
"Were she cross-grained, she could not be endured."
A word of truth from her had startled you;
But you — you claimed the universe; nought less
Than all existence working in sure tracks
Towards your supremacy. The wheels might scathe
A myriad destinies — nay, must perforce;
But yours they must keep clear of; just for you
The seething atoms through the firmament
Must bear a human heart — which you had not!
For what is it to you that women, men,

Plod, faint, are weary, and espouse despair
Of aught but fellowship? Save that you spurn
To be among them? Now, then, you are lame —
Maimed, as you said, and levelled with the crowd:
Call it new birth — birth from that monstrous Self
Which, smiling down upon a race oppressed,
Says, "All is good, for I am throned at ease."
Dear Armgart — nay, you tremble — I am cruel.

ARMGART.

Oh no! hark! Some one knocks. Come in! — come in!

(*Enter* LEO.)

LEO.

See, Gretchen let me in. I could not rest
Longer away from you.

ARMGART.

Sit down, dear Leo.
Walpurga, I would speak with him alone.

(WALPURGA *goes out.*)

LEO (*hesitatingly*).

You mean to walk?

ARMGART.

No, I shall stay within.

(*She takes off her hat and mantle, and sits down immediately. After a pause, speaking in a subdued tone to* LEO.)

How old are you?

LEO.

Threescore and five.

ARMGART.

That's old.

I never thought till now how you have lived.

They hardly ever play your music?

LEO (*raising his eyebrows, and throwing out his lip.*)

No!

Schubert too wrote for silence: half his work
Lay like a frozen Rhine till summers came
That warmed the grass above him. Even so!
His music lives now with a mighty youth.

ARMGART.

Do you think yours will live when you are dead?

LEO.

Pfui! The time was, I drank that home-brewed wine
And found it heady, while my blood was young:
Now it scarce warms me. Tipple it as I may,
I am sober still, and say: "My old friend Leo,
Much grain is wasted in the world and rots;
Why not thy handful?"

ARMGART.

Strange! since I have known you
Till now I never wondered how you lived.
When I sang well — that was your jubilee.
But you were old already.

LEO.

Yes, child, yes:
Youth thinks itself the goal of each old life;
Age has but travelled from a far-off time
Just to be ready for youth's service. Well!
It was my chief delight to perfect you.

ARMGART.

Good Leo! You have lived on little joys.
But your delight in me is crushed forever.
Your pains, where are they now? They shaped intent
Which action frustrates; shaped an inward sense
Which is but keen despair, the agony
Of highest vision in the lowest pit.

LEO.

Nay, nay, I have a thought: keep to the stage,
To drama without song; for you can act —
Who knows how well, when all the soul is poured
Into that sluice alone?

ARMGART.

I know, and you:
The second or third best in tragedies
That cease to touch the fibre of the time.
No; song is gone, but nature's other gift,
Self-judgment, is not gone. Song was my speech,
And with its impulse only, action came:
Song was the battle's onset, when cool purpose
Glows into rage, becomes a warring god
And moves the limbs with miracle. But now —
Oh, I should stand hemmed in with thoughts and rules —
Say "This way passion acts," yet never feel
The might of passion. How should I declaim?
As monsters write with feet instead of hands.
I will not feed on doing great tasks ill,
Dull the world's sense with mediocrity,
And live by trash that smothers excellence.
One gift I had that ranked me with the best·
The secret of my frame — and that is gone.
For all life now I am a broken thing.

But silence there! Good Leo, advise me now.
I would take humble work and do it well —
Teach music, singing — what I can — not here,
But in some smaller town where I may bring
The method you have taught me, pass your gift
To others who can use it for delight.
You think I can do that?

(*She pauses with a sob in her voice.*)

LEO.

Yes, yes, dear child!
And it were well, perhaps, to change the place —
Begin afresh as I did when I left
Vienna with a heart half broken.

ARMGART (*roused by surprise*).

You?

LEO.

Well, it is long ago. But I had lost —
No matter! We must bury our dead joys

And live above them with a living world.
But whither, think you, you would like to go?

ARMGART.

To Freiburg.

LEO.

In the Breisgau? And why there?
It is too small.

ARMGART.

Walpurga was born there,
And loves the place. She quitted it for me
These five years past. Now I will take her there.
Dear Leo, I will bury my dead joy.

LEO.

Mothers do so, bereaved; then learn to love
Another's living child.

ARMGART.

Oh, it is hard

To take the little corpse, and lay it low,
And say, "None misses it but me."
She sings . . .
I mean Paulina sings Fidelio,
And they will welcome her to-night.

LEO.

Well, well,
'Tis better that our griefs should not spread far.

1870.

HOW LISA LOVED THE KING.

HOW LISA LOVED THE KING.

Six hundred years ago, in Dante's time,
Before his cheek was furrowed by deep rhyme—
When Europe, fed afresh from Eastern story,
Was like a garden tangled with the glory
Of flowers hand-planted and of flowers air-sown,
Climbing and trailing, budding and full-blown,
Where purple bells are tossed amid pink stars,
And springing blades, green troops in innocent wars,
Crowd every shady spot of teeming earth,
Making invisible motion visible birth—
Six hundred years ago, Palermo town
Kept holiday. A deed of great renown,
A high revenge, had freed it from the yoke
Of hated Frenchmen, and from Calpe's rock

To where the Bosphorus caught the earlier sun,
'Twas told that Pedro, King of Aragon,
Was welcomed master of all Sicily,
A royal knight, supreme as kings should be,
In strength and gentleness that make high chivalry.

Spain was the favorite home of knightly grace,
Where generous men rode steeds of generous race;
Both Spanish, yet half Arab, both inspired
By mutual spirit, that each motion fired
With beauteous response, like minstrelsy
Afresh fulfilling fresh expectancy.
So when Palermo made high festival,
The joy of matrons and of maidens all
Was the mock terror of the tournament,
Where safety, with the glimpse of danger blent,
Took exaltation as from epic song,
Which greatly tells the pains that to great life belong.
And in all eyes King Pedro was the king
Of cavaliers: as in a full-gemmed ring
The largest ruby, or as that bright star
Whose shining shows us where the Hyads are.

His the best genet, and he sat it best;
His weapon, whether tilting or in rest,
Was worthiest watching, and his face once seen
Gave to the promise of his royal mien
Such rich fulfilment as the opened eyes
Of a loved sleeper, or the long-watched rise
Of vernal day, whose joy o'er stream and meadow
flies.

But of the maiden forms that thick inwreathed
The broad piazza and sweet witchery breathed,
With innocent faces budding all arow
From balconies and windows high and low,
Who was it felt the deep mysterious glow,
The impregnation with supernal fire
Of young ideal love — transformed desire,
Whose passion is but worship of that Best
Taught by the many-mingled creed of each young
breast?

'Twas gentle Lisa, of no noble line,
Child of Bernardo, a rich Florentine,

Who from his merchant-city hither came
To trade in drugs ; yet kept an honest fame,
And had the virtue not to try and sell
Drugs that had none. He loved his riches well,
But loved them chiefly for his Lisa's sake,
Whom with a father's care he sought to make
The bride of some true honorable man : —
Of Perdicone (so the rumor ran),
Whose birth was higher than his fortunes were ;
For still your trader likes a mixture fair
Of blood that hurries to some higher strain
Than reckoning money's loss and money's gain.
And of such mixture good may surely come :
Lords' scions so may learn to cast a sum,
A trader's grandson bear a well-set head,
And have less conscious manners, better bred ;
Nor, when he tries to be polite, be rude instead.

'Twas Perdicone's friends made overtures
To good Bernardo ; so one dame assures
Her neighbor dame who notices the youth
Fixing his eyes on Lisa ; and in truth

Eyes that could see her on this summer day
Might find it hard to turn another way.
She had a pensive beauty, yet not sad;
Rather, like minor cadences that glad
The hearts of little birds amid spring boughs;
And oft the trumpet or the joust would rouse
Pulses that gave her cheek a finer glow,
Parting her lips that seemed a mimic bow
By chiselling Love for play in coral wrought,
Then quickened by him with the passionate thought,
The soul that trembled in the lustrous night
Of slow long eyes. Her body was so slight,
It seemed she could have floated in the sky,
And with the angelic choir made symphony;
But in her cheek's rich tinge, and in the dark
Of darkest hair and eyes, she bore a mark
Of kinship to her generous mother earth,
The fervid land that gives the plumy palm-trees
birth.

She saw not Perdicone; her young mind
Dreamed not that any man had ever pined

For such a little simple maid as she:
She had but dreamed how heavenly it would be
To love some hero noble, beauteous, great,
Who would live stories worthy to narrate,
Like Roland, or the warriors of Troy,
The Cid, or Amadis, or that fair boy
Who conquered every thing beneath the sun,
And somehow, some time, died at Babylon
Fighting the Moors. For heroes all were good
And fair as that archangel who withstood
The Evil One, the author of all wrong —
That Evil One who made the French so strong;
And now the flower of heroes must be he
Who drove those tyrants from dear Sicily,
So that her maids might walk to vespers tranquilly.

Young Lisa saw this hero in the king,
And as wood-lilies that sweet odors bring
Might dream the light that opes their modest eyne
Was lily-odored, — and as rites divine,
Round turf-laid altars, or 'neath roofs of stone,
Draw sanctity from out the heart alone

That loves and worships, so the miniature
Perplexed of her soul's world, all virgin pure,
Filled with heroic virtues that bright form,
Raona's royalty, the finished norm
Of horsemanship — the half of chivalry:
For how could generous men avengers be,
Save as God's messengers on coursers fleet? —
These, scouring earth, made Spain with Syria meet
In one self world where the same right had sway,
And good must grow as grew the blessed day.
No more; great Love his essence had endued
With Pedro's form, and entering subdued
The soul of Lisa, fervid and intense,
Proud in its choice of proud obedience
To hardship glorified by perfect reverence.

Sweet Lisa homeward carried that dire guest,
And in her chamber through the hours of rest
The darkness was alight for her with sheen
Of arms, and plumèd helm, and bright between
Their commoner gloss, like the pure living spring

'Twixt porphyry lips, or living bird's bright wing
'Twixt golden wires, the glances of the king
Flashed on her soul, and waked vibrations there
Of known delights love-mixed to new and rare:
The impalpable dream was turned to breathing flesh,
Chill thought of summer to the warm close mesh
Of sunbeams held between the citron-leaves,
Clothing her life of life. Oh, she believes
That she could be content if he but knew
(Her poor small self could claim no other due)
How Lisa's lowly love had highest reach
Of wingèd passion, whereto wingèd speech
Would be scorched remnants left by mounting flame.
Though, had she such lame message, were it blame
To tell what greatness dwelt in her, what rank
She held in loving? Modest maidens shrank
From telling love that fed on selfish hope;
But love, as hopeless as the shattering song
Wailed for loved beings who have joined the throng
Of mighty dead ones. . . .Nay, but she was weak —
Knew only prayers and ballads — could not speak

With eloquence save what dumb creatures have,
That with small cries and touches small boons
crave.

She watched all day that she might see him pass
With knights and ladies; but she said, "Alas!
Though he should see me, it were all as one
He saw a pigeon sitting on the stone
Of wall or balcony: some colored spot
His eye just sees, his mind regardeth not.
I have no music-touch that could bring nigh
My love to his soul's hearing. I shall die,
And he will never know who Lisa was —
The trader's child, whose soaring spirit rose
As hedge-born aloe-flowers that rarest years dis-
close.

"For were I now a fair deep-breasted queen
A-horseback, with blonde hair, and tunic green
Gold-bordered, like Costanza, I should need
No change within to make me queenly there;
For they the royal-hearted women are

Who nobly love the noblest, yet have grace
For needy suffering lives in lowliest place,
Carrying a choicer sunlight in their smile,
The heavenliest ray that pitieth the vile.
My love is such, it cannot choose but soar
Up to the highest; yet forevermore,
Though I were happy, throned beside the king,
I should be tender to each little thing
With hurt warm breast, that had no speech to tell
Its inward pang, and I would soothe it well
With tender touch and with a low soft moan
For company: my dumb love-pang is lone,
Prisoned as topaz-beam within a rough-garbed stone."

So, inward-wailing, Lisa passed her days.
Each night the August moon with changing phase
Looked broader, harder on her unchanged pain;
Each noon the heat lay heavier again
On her despair; until her body frail
Shrank like the snow that watchers in the vale

See narrowed on the height each summer morn;
While her dark glance burnt larger, more forlorn,
As if the soul within her all on fire
Made of her being one swift funeral pyre.
Father and mother saw with sad dismay
The meaning of their riches melt away:
For without Lisa what would sequins buy?
What wish were left if Lisa were to die?
Through her they cared for summers still to come,
Else they would be as ghosts without a home
In any flesh that could feel glad desire.
They pay the best physicians, never tire
Of seeking what will soothe her, promising
That aught she longed for, though it were a thing
Hard to be come at as the Indian snow,
Or roses that on alpine summits blow —
It should be hers. She answers with low voice,
She longs for death alone — death is her choice;
Death is the King who never did think scorn,
But rescues every meanest soul to sorrow born.

Yet one day, as they bent above her bed
And watched her in brief sleep, her drooping head

Turned gently, as the thirsty flowers that feel
Some moist revival through their petals steal,
And little flutterings of her lids and lips
Told of such dreamy joy as sometimes dips
A skyey shadow in the mind's poor pool.
She oped her eyes, and turned their dark gems full
Upon her father, as in utterance dumb
Of some new prayer that in her sleep had come.
"What is it, Lisa?" "Father, I would see
Minuccio, the great singer; bring him me."
For always, night and day, her unstilled thought,
Wandering all o'er its little world, had sought
How she could reach, by some soft pleading touch,
King Pedro's soul, that she who loved so much
Dying, might have a place within his mind —
A little grave which he would sometimes find
And plant some flower on it — some thought, some
memory kind.
Till in her dream she saw Minuccio
Touching his viola, and chanting low,
A strain that, falling on her brokenly,
Seemed blossoms lightly blown from off a tree,

Each burthened with a word that was a scent —
Raona, Lisa, love, death, tournament;
Then in her dream she said, "He sings of me —
Might be my messenger; ah, now I see
The king is listening" — Then she awoke,
And, missing her dear dream, that new-born longing spoke.

She longed for music: that was natural;
Physicians said it was medicinal;
The humors might be schooled by true consent
Of a fine tenor and fine instrument;
In brief, good music, mixed with doctor's stuff,
Apollo with Asklepios — enough!
Minuccio, entreated, gladly came.
(He was a singer of most gentle fame —
A noble, kindly spirit, not elate
That he was famous, but that song was great —
Would sing as finely to this suffering child
As at the court where princes on him smiled.)
Gently he entered and sat down by her,
Asking what sort of strain she would prefer —

The voice alone, or voice with viol wed;
Then, when she chose the last, he preluded
With magic hand, that summoned from the strings
Aerial spirits, rare yet vibrant wings
That fanned the pulses of his listener,
And waked each sleeping sense with blissful stir.
Her cheek already showed a slow faint blush,
But soon the voice, in pure full liquid rush,
Made all the passion, that till now she felt,
Seem but cool waters that in warmer melt.
Finished the song, she prayed to be alone
With kind Minuccio; for her faith had grown
To trust him as if missioned like a priest
With some high grace, that when his singing ceased
Still made him wiser, more magnanimous
Than common men who had no genius.
So laying her small hand within his palm,
She told him how that secret glorious harm
Of loftiest loving had befallen her;
That death, her only hope, most bitter were,
If when she died her love must perish too
As songs unsung and thoughts unspoken do,

Which else might live within another breast.
She said, "Minuccio, the grave were rest,
If I were sure, that lying cold and lone,
My love, my best of life, had safely flown,
And nestled in the bosom of the king;
See, 'tis a small weak bird, with unfledged wing.
But you will carry it for me secretly,
And bear it to the king, then come to me
And tell me it is safe, and I shall go
Content, knowing that he I love my love doth know."

Then she wept silently, but each large tear
Made pleading music to the inward ear
Of good Minuccio. "Lisa, trust in me,"
He said, and kissed her fingers loyally;
"It is sweet law to me to do your will,
And ere the sun his round shall thrice fulfil,
I hope to bring you news of such rare skill
As amulets have, that aches in trusting bosoms still."

He needed not to pause and first devise
How he should tell the king; for in no wise
Were such love-message worthily bested
Save in fine verse by music renderèd.
He sought a poet-friend, a Siennese,
And "Mico, mine," he said, "full oft to please
Thy whim of sadness I have sung thee strains
To make thee weep in verse: now pay my pains,
And write me a canzone divinely sad,
Sinlessly passionate and meekly mad
With young despair, speaking a maiden's heart
Of fifteen summers, who would fain depart
From ripening life's new-urgent mystery—
Love-choice of one too high her love to be—
But cannot yield her breath till she has poured
Her strength away in this hot-bleeding word,
Telling the secret of her soul to her soul's lord."

Said Mico, "Nay, that thought is poesy,
I need but listen as it sings to me.
Come thou again to-morrow." The third day,
When linkèd notes had perfected the lay,

Minuccio had his summons to the court
To make, as he was wont, the moments short
Of ceremonious dinner to the king.
This was the time when he had meant to bring
Melodious message of young Lisa's love:
He waited till the air had ceased to move
To ringing silver, till Falernian wine
Made quickened sense with quietude combine,
And then with passionate descant made each ear incline.

Love, thou didst see me, light as morning's breath,
Roaming a garden in a joyous error,
Laughing at chases vain, a happy child,
Till of thy countenance the alluring terror
In majesty from out the blossoms smiled,
From out their life seeming a beauteous Death.

O Love, who so didst choose me for thine own,
Taking this little isle to thy great sway,
See now, it is the honor of thy throne
That what thou gavest perish not away,

Nor leave some sweet remembrance to atone
By life that will be for the brief life gone:
Here, ere the shroud o'er these frail limbs be thrown—
Since every king is vassal unto thee,
My heart's lord needs must listen loyally—
O tell him I am waiting for my Death!

Tell him, for that he hath such royal power
'Twere hard for him to think how small a thing,
How slight a sign, would make a wealthy dower
For one like me, the bride of that pale king
Whose bed is mine at some swift-nearing hour.
Go to my lord, and to his memory bring
That happy birthday of my sorrowing
When his large glance made meaner gazers glad,
Entering the bannered lists: 'twas then I had
The wound that laid me in the arms of Death.

Tell him, O Love, I am a lowly maid,
No more than any little knot of thyme
That he with careless foot may often tread;
Yet lowest fragrance oft will mount sublime

And cleave to things most high and hallowèd,
As doth the fragrance of my life's springtime,
My lowly love, that soaring seeks to climb
Within his thought, and make a gentle bliss,
More blissful than if mine, in being his:
So shall I live in him and rest in Death.

The strain was new. It seemed a pleading cry,
And yet a rounded perfect melody,
Making grief beauteous as the tear-filled eyes
Of little child at little miseries.
Trembling at first, then swelling as it rose,
Like rising light that broad and broader grows,
It filled the hall, and so possessed the air
That not one breathing soul was present there,
Though dullest, slowest, but was quivering
In music's grasp, and forced to hear her sing.
But most such sweet compulsion took the mood
Of Pedro (tired of doing what he would).
Whether the words which that strange meaning bore
Were but the poet's feigning, or aught more,

Was bounden question, since their aim must be
At some imagined or true royalty.
He called Minuccio and bade him tell
What poet of the day had writ so well;
For though they came behind all former rhymes,
The verses were not bad for these poor times.

"Monsignor, they are only three days old,"
Minuccio said; "but it must not be told
How this song grew, save to your royal ear."
Eager, the king withdrew where none was near,
And gave close audience to Minuccio,
Who meetly told that love-tale meet to know.
The king had features pliant to confess
The presence of a manly tenderness —
Son, father, brother, lover, blent in one,
In fine harmonic exaltation —
The spirit of religious chivalry.
He listened, and Minuccio could see
The tender, generous admiration spread
O'er all his face, and glorify his head
With royalty that would have kept its rank
Though his brocaded robes to tatters shrank.

He answered without pause, " So sweet a maid,
In nature's own insignia arrayed,
Though she were come of unmixed trading blood
That sold and bartered ever since the Flood,
Would have the self-contained and single worth
Of radiant jewels born in darksome earth.
Raona were a shame to Sicily,
Letting such love and tears unhonored be:
Hasten, Minuccio, tell her that the king
To-day will surely visit her when vespers ring."

Joyful, Minuccio bore the joyous word,
And told at full, while none but Lisa heard,
How each thing had befallen, sang the song,
And like a patient nurse who would prolong
All means of soothing, dwelt upon each tone,
Each look, with which the mighty Aragon
Marked the high worth his royal heart assigned
To that dear place he held in Lisa's mind.
She listened till the draughts of pure content
Through all her limbs like some new being went —
Life, not recovered, but untried before,
From out the growing world's unmeasured store

Of fuller, better, more divinely mixed.
'Twas glad reverse: she had so firmly fixed
To die, already seemed to fall a veil
Shrouding the inner glow from light of senses pale.

Her parents wondering see her half arise —
Wondering, rejoicing, see her long dark eyes
Brimful with clearness, not of 'scaping tears,
But of some light ethereal that enspheres
Their orbs with calm, some vision newly learnt
Where strangest fires erewhile had blindly burnt.
She asked to have her soft white robe and band
And coral ornaments, and with her hand
She gave her locks' dark length a backward fall,
Then looked intently in a mirror small,
And feared her face might perhaps displease the
king;
"In truth," she said, "I am a tiny thing;
I was too bold to tell what could such visit bring."

Meanwhile the king, revolving in his thought
That virgin passion, was more deeply wrought

To chivalrous pity; and at vesper bell,
With careless mien which hid his purpose well,
Went forth on horseback, and as if by chance
Passing Bernardo's house, he paused to glance
At the fine garden of this wealthy man,
This Tuscan trader turned Palermitan:
But, presently dismounting, chose to walk
Amid the trellises, in gracious talk
With this same trader, deigning even to ask
If he had yet fulfilled the father's task
Of marrying that daughter whose young charms
Himself, betwixt the passages of arms,
Noted admiringly. "Monsignor, no,
She is not married; that were little woe,
Since she has counted barely fifteen years;
But all such hopes of late have turned to fears;
She droops and fades; though for a space quite brief—
Scarce three hours past—she finds some strange relief."
The king advised: "Twere dole to all of us,
The world should lose a maid so beauteous;

Let me now see her; since I am her liege lord,
Her spirits must wage war with death at my strong
word."
In such half-serious playfulness, he wends,
With Lisa's father and two chosen friends,
Up to the chamber where she pillowed sits
Watching the opened door, that now admits
A presence as much better than her dreams,
As happiness than any longing seems.
The king advanced, and, with a reverent kiss
Upon her hand, said, "Lady, what is this?
You, whose sweet youth should others' solace be,
Pierce all our hearts, languishing piteously.
We pray you, for the love of us, be cheered,
Nor be too reckless of that life, endeared
To us who know your passing worthiness,
And count your blooming life as part of our life's
bliss."

Those words, that touch upon her hand from him
Whom her soul worshipped, as far seraphim
Worship the distant glory, brought some shame
Quivering upon her cheek, yet thrilled her frame

With such deep joy she seemed in paradise,
In wondering gladness, and in dumb surprise
That bliss could be so blissful: then she spoke —
"Signor, I was too weak to bear the yoke,
The golden yoke of thoughts too great for me;
That was the ground of my infirmity.
But now, I pray your grace to have belief
That I shall soon be well, nor any more cause
grief."

The king alone perceived the covert sense
Of all her words, which made one evidence
With her pure voice and candid loveliness,
That he had lost much honor, honoring less
That message of her passionate distress.
He staid beside her for a little while
With gentle looks and speech, until a smile
As placid as a ray of early morn
On opening flower-cups o'er her lips was borne.
When he had left her, and the tidings spread
Through all the town how he had visited
The Tuscan trader's daughter, who was sick,
Men said, it was a royal deed and catholic.

And Lisa? she no longer wished for death;
But as a poet, who sweet verses saith
Within his soul, and joys in music there,
Nor seeks another heaven, nor can bear
Disturbing pleasures, so was she content,
Breathing the life of grateful sentiment.
She thought no maid betrothed could be more blest;
For treasure must be valued by the test
Of highest excellence and rarity,
And her dear joy was best as best could be;
There seemed no other crown to her delight
Now the high loved one saw her love aright.
Thus her soul thriving on that exquisite mood,
Spread like the May-time all its beauteous good
O'er the soft bloom of neck, and arms, and cheek,
And strengthened the sweet body, once so weak,
Until she rose and walked, and, like a bird
With sweetly rippling throat, she made her spring
joys heard.

The king, when he the happy change had seen,
Trusted the ear of Constance, his fair queen,

With Lisa's innocent secret, and conferred
How they should jointly, by their deed and word,
Honor this maiden's love, which, like the prayer
Of loyal hermits, never thought to share
In what it gave. The queen had that chief grace
Of womanhood, a heart that can embrace
All goodness in another woman's form;
And that same day, ere the sun lay too warm
On southern terraces, a messenger
Informed Bernardo that the royal pair
Would straightway visit him, and celebrate
Their gladness at his daughter's happier state,
Which they were fain to see. Soon came the king
On horseback, with his barons, heralding
The advent of the queen in courtly state;
And all, descending at the garden gate,
Streamed with their feathers, velvet, and brocade,
Through the pleached alleys, till they, pausing, made
A lake of splendor 'mid the aloes gray —
When, meekly facing all their proud array,
The white-robed Lisa with her parents stood,
As some white dove before the gorgeous brood
Of dapple-breasted birds born by the Colchian flood.

The king and queen, by gracious looks and speech,
Encourage her, and thus their courtiers teach
How this fair morning they may courtliest be
By making Lisa pass it happily.
And soon the ladies and the barons all
Draw her by turns, as at a festival
Made for her sake, to easy, gay discourse,
And compliment with looks and smiles enforce;
A joyous hum is heard the gardens round;
Soon there is Spanish dancing and the sound
Of minstrel's song, and autumn fruits are plucked;
Till mindfully the king and queen conduct
Lisa apart to where a trellised shade
Made pleasant resting. Then King Pedro said—
"Excellent maiden, that rich gift of love
Your heart hath made us, hath a worth above
All royal treasures, nor is fitly met
Save when the grateful memory of deep debt
Lies still behind the outward honors done:
And as a sign that no oblivion
Shall overflood that faithful memory,
We while we live your cavalier will be,

Nor will we ever arm ourselves for fight,
Whether for struggle dire or brief delight
Of warlike feigning, but we first will take
The colors you ordain, and for your sake
Charge the more bravely where your emblem is;
Nor will we ever claim an added bliss
To our sweet thoughts of you save one sole kiss.
But there still rests the outward honor meet
To mark your worthiness, and we entreat
That you will turn your ear to proffered vows
Of one who loves you, and would be your spouse.
We must not wrong yourself and Sicily
By letting all your blooming years pass by
Unmated: you will give the world its due
From beauteous maiden and become a matron true."

Then Lisa, wrapt in virgin wonderment
At her ambitious love's complete content,
Which left no further good for her to seek
Than love's obedience, said with accent meek—
"Monsignor, I know well that were it known
To all the world how high my love had flown,

There would be few who would not deem me mad,
Or say my mind the falsest image had
Of my condition and your lofty place.
But Heaven has seen that for no moment's space
Have I forgotten you to be the king,
Or me myself to be a lowly thing —
A little bark, enamoured of the sky,
That soared to sing, to break its breast, and die.
But, as you better know than I, the heart
In choosing chooseth not its own desert,
But that great merit which attracteth it;
'Tis law, I struggled, but I must submit,
And having seen a worth all worth above,
I loved you, love you, and shall always love.
But that doth mean, my will is ever yours,
Not only when your will my good insures,
But if it wrought me what the world calls narm —
Fire, wounds, would wear from your dear will a
charm.
That you will be my knight is full content,
And for that kiss — I pray, first for the queen's
consent."

Her answer, given with such firm gentleness,
Pleased the queen well, and made her hold no less
Of Lisa's merit than the king had held.
And so, all cloudy threats of grief dispelled,
There was betrothal made that very morn
'Twixt Perdicone, youthful, brave, well-born,
And Lisa, whom he loved; she loving well
The lot that from obedience befell.
The queen a rare betrothal ring on each
Bestowed, and other gems, with gracious speech.
And that no joy might lack, the king, who knew
The youth was poor, gave him rich Ceffalù
And Cataletta, large and fruitful lands —
Adding much promise when he joined their hands.
At last he said to Lisa, with an air
Gallant yet noble: "Now we claim our share
From your sweet love, a share which is not small:
For in the sacrament one crumb is all."
Then taking her small face his hands between,
He kissed her on the brow with kiss serene,
Fit seal to that pure vision her young soul had
seen.

Sicilians witnessed that King Pedro kept
His royal promise: Perdicone stept
To many honors honorably won,
Living with Lisa in true union.
Throughout his life the king still took delight
To call himself fair Lisa's faithful knight;
And never wore in field or tournament
A scarf or emblem save by Lisa sent.

Such deeds made subjects loyal in that land:
They joyed that one so worthy to command,
So chivalrous and gentle, had become
The king of Sicily, and filled the room
Of Frenchmen, who abused the Church's trust,
Till, in a righteous vengeance on their lust,
Messina rose, with God, and with the dagger's thrust.

L'ENVOI.

Reader, this story pleased me long ago
In the bright pages of Boccaccio,
And where the author of a good we know,
Let us not fail to pay the grateful thanks we owe.

1869.

A MINOR PROPHET.

A MINOR PROPHET.

I HAVE a friend, a vegetarian seer,
By name Elias Baptist Butterworth,
A harmless, bland, disinterested man,
Whose ancestors in Cromwell's day believed
The Second Advent certain in five years,
But when King Charles the Second came instead,
Revised their date and sought another world:
I mean — not heaven but — America.
A fervid stock, whose generous hope embraced
The fortunes of mankind, not stopping short
At rise of leather, or the fall of gold,
Nor listening to the voices of the time
As housewives listen to a cackling hen,
With wonder whether she has laid her egg

On their own nest-egg. Still they did insist
Somewhat too wearisomely on the joys
Of their Millennium, when coats and hats
Would all be of one pattern, books and songs
All fit for Sundays, and the casual talk
As good as sermons preached extempore.

And in Elias the ancestral zeal
Breathes strong as ever, only modified
By Transatlantic air and modern thought.
You could not pass him in the street and fail
To note his shoulders' long declivity,
Beard to the waist, swan-neck, and large pale eyes;
Or, when he lifts his hat, to mark his hair
Brushed back to show his great capacity —
A full grain's length at the angle of the brow
Proving him witty, while the shallower men
Only seem witty in their repartees.
Not that he's vain, but that his doctrine needs
The testimony of his frontal lobe.
On all points he adopts the latest views;
Takes for the key of universal Mind

The "levitation" of stout gentlemen;
Believes the Rappings are not spirits' work,
But the Thought-atmosphere's, a steam of brains
In correlated force of raps, as proved
By motion, heat, and science generally;
The spectrum, for example, which has shown
The selfsame metals in the sun as here;
So the Thought-atmosphere is everywhere:
High truths that glimmered under other names
To ancient sages, whence good scholarship
Applied to Eleusinian mysteries —
The Vedas — Tripitaka — Vendidad —
Might furnish weaker proof for weaker minds
That Thought was rapping in the hoary past,
And might have edified the Greeks by raps
At the greater Dionysia, if their ears
Had not been filled with Sophoclean verse.
And when all Earth is vegetarian —
When, lacking butchers, quadrupeds die out,
And less Thought-atmosphere is re-absorbed
By nerves of insects parasitical,
Those higher truths, seized now by higher minds

But not expressed (the insects hindering)
Will either flash out into eloquence,
Or better still, be comprehensible
By rappings simply, without need of roots.

'Tis on this theme — the vegetarian world —
That good Elias willingly expands:
He loves to tell in mildly nasal tones
And vowels stretched to suit the widest views,
The future fortunes of our infant Earth —
When it will be too full of human kind
To have the room for wilder animals.
Saith he, Sahara will be populous
With families of gentlemen retired
From commerce in more Central Africa,
Who order coolness as we order coal,
And have a lobe anterior strong enougn
To think away the sand-storms. Science thus
Will leave no spot on this terraqueous globe
Unfit to be inhabited by man,
The chief of animals: all meaner brutes
Will have been smoked and elbowed out of life.

No lions then shall lap Caffrarian pools,
Or shake the Atlas with their midnight roar:
Even the slow, slime-loving crocodile,
The last of animals to take a hint,
Will then retire forever from a scene
Where public feeling strongly sets against him.
Fishes may lead carnivorous lives obscure,
But must not dream of culinary rank
Or being dished in good society.
Imagination in that distant age,
Aiming at fiction called historical,
Will vainly try to reconstruct the times
When it was men's preposterous delight
To sit astride live horses, which consumed
Materials for incalculable cakes;
When there were milkmaids who drew milk from cows
With udders kept abnormal for that end
Since the rude mythopœic period
Of Aryan dairymen, who did not blush
To call their milkmaid and their daughter one —
Helplessly gazing at the Milky Way,

Nor dreaming of the astral cocoanuts
Quite at the service of posterity.
'Tis to be feared, though, that the duller boys,
Much given to anachronisms and nuts,
(Elias has confessed boys will be boys)
May write a jockey for a centaur, think
Europa's suitor was an Irish bull,
Æsop a journalist who wrote up Fox,
And Bruin a chief swindler upon 'Change.
Boys will be boys, but dogs will all be moral,
With longer alimentary canals
Suited to diet vegetarian.
The uglier breeds will fade from memory,
Or, being paleontological,
Live but as portraits in large learned books,
Distasteful to the feelings of an age
Nourished on purest beauty. Earth will hold
No stupid brutes, no cheerful queernesses,
No naïve cunning, grave absurdity.
Wart-pigs with tender and parental grunts,
Wombats much flattened as to their contour,
Perhaps from too much crushing in the ark,

But taking meekly that fatality;
The serious cranes, unstung by ridicule;
Long-headed, short-legged, solemn-looking curs,
(Wise, silent critics of a flippant age);
The silly straddling foals, the weak-brained geese
Hissing fallaciously at sound of wheels —
All these rude products will have disappeared
Along with every faulty human type.
By dint of diet vegetarian
All will be harmony of hue and line,
Bodies and minds all perfect, limbs well-turned,
And talk quite free from aught erroneous.

Thus far Elias in his seer's mantle:
But at this climax in his prophecy
My sinking spirits, fearing to be swamped,
Urge me to speak. "High prospects, these my friend,
Setting the weak carnivorous brain astretch;
We will resume the thread another day."
"To-morrow," cries Elias, "at this hour?"
"No, not to-morrow — I shall have a cold —

At least I feel some soreness — this endemic —
Good-by."
No tears are sadder than the smile
With which I quit Elias. Bitterly
I feel that every change upon this earth
Is bought with sacrifice. My yearnings fail
To reach that high apocalyptic mount
Which shows in bird's-eye view a perfect world,
Or enter warmly into other joys
Than those of faulty, struggling human kind.
That strain upon my soul's too feeble wing
Ends in ignoble floundering: I fall
Into short-sighted pity for the men
Who living in those perfect future times
Will not know half the dear imperfect things
That move my smiles and tears — will never know
The fine old incongruities that raise
My friendly laugh; the innocent conceits
That like a needless eyeglass or black patch
Give those who wear them harmless happiness;
The twists and cracks in our poor earthenware,
That touch me to more conscious fellowship

(I am not myself the finest Parian)
With my coevals. So poor Colin Clout,
To whom raw onion gives prospective zest,
Consoling hours of dampest wintry work,
Could hardly fancy any regal joys
Quite unimpregnate with the onion's scent:
Perhaps his highest hopes are not all clear
Of waftings from that energetic bulb:
'Tis well that onion is not heresy.
Speaking in parable, I am Colin Clout.
A clinging flavor penetrates my life —
My onion is imperfectness: I cleave
To nature's blunders, evanescent types
Which sages banish from Utopia.
"Not worship beauty?" say you. Patience, friend!
I worship in the temple with the rest;
But by my hearth I keep a sacred nook
For gnomes and dwarfs, duck-footed waddling elves
Who stitched and hammered for the weary man
In days of old. And in that piety
I clothe ungainly forms inherited
From toiling generations, daily bent

At desk, or plough, or loom, or in the mine,
In pioneering labors for the world.
Nay, I am apt when floundering confused
From too rash flight, to grasp at paradox,
And pity future men who will not know
A keen experience with pity blent,
The pathos exquisite of lovely minds
Hid in harsh forms — not penetrating them
Like fire divine within a common bush
Which glows transfigured by the heavenly guest,
So that men put their shoes off ; but incaged
Like a sweet child within some thick-walled cell,
Who leaps and fails to hold the window-bars,
But having shown a little dimpled hand
Is visited thenceforth by tender hearts
Whose eyes keep watch about the prison walls.
A foolish, nay, a wicked paradox!
For purest pity is the eye of love
Melting at sight of sorrow ; and to grieve
Because it sees no sorrow, shows a love
Warped from its truer nature, turned to love
Of merest habit, like the miser's greed.

But I am Colin still: my prejudice
Is for the flavor of my daily food.
Not that I doubt the world is growing still
As once it grew from Chaos and from Night;
Or have a soul too shrunken for the hope
Which dawned in human breasts, a double morn,
With earliest watchings of the rising light
Chasing the darkness; and through many an age
Has raised the vision of a future time
That stands an Angel with a face all mild
Spearing the demon. I too rest in faith
That man's perfection is the crowning flower,
Toward which the urgent sap in life's great tree
Is pressing, — seen in puny blossoms now,
But in the world's great morrows to expand
With broadest petal and with deepest glow.

Yet, see the patched and plodding citizen
Waiting upon the pavement with the throng
While some victorious world-hero makes
Triumphal entry, and the peal of shouts
And flash of faces 'neath uplifted hats

Run like a storm of joy along the streets!
He says, "God bless him!" almost with a sob,
As the great hero passes; he is glad
The world holds mighty men and mighty deeds;
The music stirs his pulses like strong wine,
The moving splendor touches him with awe—
'Tis glory shed around the common weal,
And he will pay his tribute willingly,
Though with the pennies earned by sordid toil.
Perhaps the hero's deeds have helped to bring
A time when every honest citizen
Shall wear a coat unpatched. And yet he feels
More easy fellowship with neighbors there
Who look on too; and he will soon relapse
From noticing the banners and the steeds
To think with pleasure there is just one bun
Left in his pocket, that may serve to tempt
The wide-eyed lad, whose weight is all too much
For that young mother's arms: and then he falls
To dreamy picturing of sunny days
When he himself was a small big-cheeked lad
In some far village where no heroes came,

And stood a listener 'twixt his father's legs
In the warm fire-light, while the old folk talked
And shook their heads and looked upon the floor;
And he was puzzled, thinking life was fine —
The bread and cheese so nice all through the year,
And Christmas sure to come. O that good time!
He, could he choose, would have those days again,
And see the dear old-fashioned things once more.
But soon the wheels and drums have all passed by,
And tramping feet are heard like sudden rain:
The quiet startles our good citizen;
He feels the child upon his arms, and knows
He is with the people making holiday
Because of hopes for better days to come.
But Hope to him was like the brilliant west
Telling of sunrise in a world unknown,
And from that dazzling curtain of bright hues
He turned to the familiar face of fields
Lying all clear in the calm morning land.
Maybe 'tis wiser not to fix a lens
Too scrutinizing on the glorious times
When Barbarossa shall arise and shake

His mountain, good King Arthur come again,
And all the heroes of such giant soul
That, living once to cheer mankind with hope,
They had to sleep until the time was ripe
For greater deeds to match their greater thought.
Yet no! the earth yields nothing more Divine
Than high prophetic vision — than the Seer
Who fasting from man's meaner joy beholds
The paths of beauteous order, and constructs
A fairer type, to shame our low content.
But prophecy is like potential sound
Which turned to music seems a voice sublime
From out the soul of light; but turns to noise
In scrannel pipes, and makes all ears averse.

The faith that life on earth is being shaped
To glorious ends, that order, justice, love
Mean man's completeness, mean effect as sure
As roundness in the dew-drop — that great faith
Is but the rushing and expanding stream
Of thought, of feeling, fed by all the past.
Our finest hope is finest memory,

As they who love in age think youth is blest
Because it has a life to fill with love
Full souls are double mirrors, making still
An endless vista of fair things before
Repeating things behind: so faith is strong
Only when we are strong, shrinks when we shrink.
It comes when music stirs us, and the chords
Moving on some grand climax shake our souls
With influx new that makes new energies.
It comes in swellings of the heart and tears
That rise at noble and at gentle deeds —
At labors of the master-artist's hand,
Which, trembling, touches to a finer end,
Trembling before an image seen within.
It comes in moments of heroic love,
Unjealous joy in joy not made for us —
In conscious triumph of the good within
Making us worship goodness that rebukes.
Even our failures are a prophecy,
Even our yearnings and our bitter tears
After that fair and true we cannot grasp;
As patriots who seem to die in vain
Make liberty more sacred by their pangs.

Presentiment of better things on earth
Sweeps in with every force that stirs our souls
To admiration, self-renouncing love,
Or thoughts, like light, that bind the world in one:
Sweeps like the sense of vastness, when at night
We hear the roll and dash of waves that break
Nearer and nearer with the rushing tide,
Which rises to the level of the cliff
Because the wide Atlantic rolls behind
Throbbing respondent to the far-off orbs.

1865.

BROTHER AND SISTER.

BROTHER AND SISTER.

I.

I CANNOT choose but think upon the time
When our two lives grew like two buds that kiss
At lightest thrill from the bee's swinging chime,
Because the one so near the other is.

He was the elder and a little man
Of forty inches, bound to show no dread,
And I the girl that puppy-like now ran,
Now lagged behind my brother's larger tread.

I held him wise, and when he talked to me
Of snakes and birds, and which God loved the best,
I thought his knowledge marked the boundary
Where men grew blind, though angels knew the rest.

If he said, "Hush!" I tried to hold my breath;
Wherever he said, "Come!" I stepped in faith.

II.

Long years have left their writing on my brow,
But yet the freshness and the dew-fed beam
Of those young mornings are about me now,
When we two wandered toward the far-off stream

With rod and line. Our basket held a store
Baked for us only, and I thought with joy
That I should have my share, though he had more,
Because he was the elder and a boy.

The firmaments of daisies since to me
Have had those mornings in their opening eyes,
The bunchèd cowslip's pale transparency
Carries that sunshine of sweet memories,

And wild-rose branches take their finest scent
From those blest hours of infantine content.

III.

Our mother bade us keep the trodden ways,
Stroked down my tippet, set my brother's frill,
Then with the benediction of her gaze
Clung to us lessening, and pursued us still

Across the homestead to the rookery elms,
Whose tall old trunks had each a grassy mound,
So rich for us, we counted them as realms
With varied products: here were earth-nuts found,

And here the Lady-fingers in deep shade;
Here sloping toward the Moat the rushes grew,
The large to split for pith, the small to braid;
While over all the dark rooks cawing flew,

And made a happy strange solemnity,
A deep-toned chant from life unknown to me.

IV.

Our meadow-path had memorable spots:
One where it bridged a tiny rivulet,
Deep hid by tangled blue Forget-me-nots;
And all along the waving grasses met

My little palm, or nodded to my cheek,
When flowers with upturned faces gazing drew
My wonder downward, seeming all to speak
With eyes of souls that dumbly heard and knew.

Then came the copse, where wild things rushed unseen,
And black-scathed grass betrayed the past abode
Of mystic gypsies, who still lurked between
Me and each hidden distance of the road.

A gypsy once had startled me at play,
Blotting with her dark smile my sunny day.

V.

Thus rambling we were schooled in deepest lore,
And learned the meanings that give words a soul,
The fear, the love, the primal passionate store,
Whose shaping impulses make manhood whole.

Those hours were seed to all my after good;
My infant gladness, through eye, ear, and touch,
Took easily as warmth a various food
To nourish the sweet skill of loving much.

For who in age shall roam the earth, and find
Reasons for loving that will strike out love
With sudden rod from the hard year-pressed mind?
Were reasons sown as thick as stars above,

'Tis love must see them, as the eye sees light:
Day is but Number to the darkened sight.

VI.

Our brown canal was endless to my thought;
And on its banks I sat in dreamy peace,
Unknowing how the good I loved was wrought,
Untroubled by the fear that it would cease.

Slowly the barges floated into view
Rounding a grassy hill to me sublime
With some Unknown beyond it, whither flew
The parting cuckoo toward a fresh spring time.

The wide-arched bridge, the scented elder-flowers,
The wondrous watery rings that died too soon,
The echoes of the quarry, the still hours
With white robe sweeping on the shadeless noon,

Were but my growing self, are part of me,
My present Past, my root of piety.

VII.

Those long days measured by my little feet
Had chronicles which yield me many a text;
Where irony still finds an image meet
Of full-grown judgments in this world perplext.

One day my brother left me in high charge,
To mind the rod, while he went seeking bait,
And bade me, when I saw a nearing barge,
Snatch out the line, lest he should come too late.

Proud of the task, I watched with all my might
For one whole minute, till my eyes grew wide,
Till sky and earth took on a strange new light
And seemed a dream-world floating on some tide —

A fair pavilioned boat for me alone
Bearing me onward through the vast unknown.

VIII.

But sudden came the barge's pitch-black prow,
Nearer and angrier came my brother's cry,
And all my soul was quivering fear, when lo!
Upon the imperilled line, suspended high,

A silver perch! My guilt that won the prey,
Now turned to merit, had a guerdon rich
Of songs and praises, and made merry play,
Until my triumph reached its highest pitch

When all at home were told the wondrous feat,
And how the little sister had fished well.
In secret, though my fortune tasted sweet,
I wondered why this happiness befell.

"The little lass had luck," the gardener said:
And so I learned, luck was with glory wed.

IX.

We had the selfsame world enlarged for each
By loving difference of girl and boy:
The fruit that hung on high beyond my reach
He plucked for me, and oft he must employ

A measuring glance to guide my tiny shoe
Where lay firm stepping-stones, or call to mind
"This thing I like my sister may not do,
For she is little, and I must be kind."

Thus boyish Will the nobler mastery learned
Where inward vision over impulse reigns,
Widening its life with separate life discerned,
A Like unlike, a Self that self restrains.

His years with others must the sweeter be
For those brief days he spent in loving me.

X.

His sorrow was my sorrow, and his joy
Sent little leaps and laughs through all my frame;
My doll seemed lifeless and no girlish toy
Had any reason when my brother came.

I knelt with him at marbles, marked his fling
Cut the ringed stem and make the apple drop,
Or watched him winding close the spiral string
That looped the orbits of the humming top.

Grasped by such fellowship my vagrant thought
Ceased with dream-fruit dream-wishes to fulfil;
My aëry-picturing fantasy was taught
Subjection to the harder, truer skill

That seeks with deeds to grave a thought-tracked line,
And by "What is," "What will be" to define.

XI.

School parted us; we never found again
That childish world where our two spirits mingled
Like scents from varying roses that remain
One sweetness, nor can evermore be singled.

Yet the twin habit of that early time
Lingered for long about the heart and tongue:
We had been natives of one happy clime
And its dear accent to our utterance clung.

Till the dire years whose awful name is Change
Had grasped our souls still yearning in divorce,
And pitiless shaped them in two forms that range
Two elements which sever their life's course.

But were another childhood-world my share,
I would be born a little sister there.

1869.

STRADIVARIUS.

STRADIVARIUS.

YOUR soul was lifted by the wings to-day
Hearing the master of the violin:
You praised him, praised the great Sebastian too
Who made that fine Chaconne; but did you think
Of old Antonio Stradivari? — him
Who a good century and half ago
Put his true work in that brown instrument,
And by the nice adjustment of its frame
Gave it responsive life, continuous
With the master's finger-tips and perfected
Like them by delicate rectitude of use.
Not Bach alone, helped by fine precedent
Of genius gone before, nor Joachim
Who holds the strain afresh incorporate

By inward hearing and notation strict
Of nerve and muscle, made our joy to-day:
Another soul was living in the air,
And swaying it to true deliverance
Of high invention and responsive skill: —
That plain white-aproned man who stood at work
Patient and accurate full fourscore years,
Cherished his sight and touch by temperance,
And since keen sense is love of perfectness
Made perfect violins, the needed paths
For inspiration and high mastery.

No simpler man than he: he never cried,
"Why was I born to this monotonous task
Of making violins?" or flung them down
To suit with hurling act a well-hurled curse
At labor on such perishable stuff.
Hence neighbors in Cremona held him dull,
Called him a slave, a mill-horse, a machine,
Begged him to tell his motives, or to lend
A few gold-pieces to a loftier mind.
Yet he had pithy words full fed by fact;

For Fact, well-trusted, reasons and persuades,
Is gnomic, cutting, or ironical,
Draws tears, or is a tocsin to arouse —
Can hold all figures of the orator
In one plain sentence; has her pauses too —
Eloquent silence at the chasm abrupt
Where knowledge ceases. Thus Antonio
Made answers as Fact willed, and made them strong.

Naldo, a painter of eclectic school,
Taking his dicers, candlelight and grins
From Caravaggio, and in holier groups
Combining Flemish flesh with martyrdom —
Knowing all tricks of style at thirty-one,
And weary of them, while Antonio
At sixty-nine wrought placidly his best
Making the violin you heard to-day —
Naldo would tease him oft to tell his aims.

"Perhaps thou hast some pleasant vice to feed —
The love of louis d'ors in heaps of four,
Each violin a heap — I've nought to blame;

My vices waste such heaps. But then, why work
With painful nicety? Since fame once earned
By luck or merit — oftenest by luck —
(Else why do I put Bonifazio's name
To work that '*pinxit Naldo*' would not sell?)
Is welcome index to the wealthy mob
Where they should pay their gold, and where they
pay
There they find merit — take your tow for flax,
And hold the flax unlabelled with your name,
Too coarse for sufferance."

Antonio then:

"I like the gold — well, yes — but not for meals.
And as my stomach, so my eye and hand,
And inward sense that works along with both,
Have hunger that can never feed on coin.
Who draws a line and satisfies his soul,
Making it crooked where it should be straight?
An idiot with an oyster-shell may draw
His lines along the sand, all wavering,
Fixing no point or pathway to a point;
An idiot one remove may choose his line,

Straggle and be content; but God be praised,
Antonio Stradivari has an eye
That winces at false work, and loves the true,
With hand and arm that play upon the tool
As willingly as any singing bird
Sets him to sing his morning roundelay,
Because he likes to sing and likes the song."

Then Naldo: "'Tis a petty kind of fame
At best, that comes of making violins;
And saves no masses, either. Thou wilt go
To purgatory none the less."

But he:

"'Twere purgatory here to make them ill;
And for my fame — when any master holds,
'Twixt chin and hand a violin of mine,
He will be glad that Stradivari lived,
Made violins, and made them of the best.
The masters only know whose work is good:
They will choose mine, and while God gives them skill
I give them instruments to play upon,
God choosing me to help Him."

"What! were God
At fault for violins, thou absent?"
"Yes;
He were at fault for Stradivari's work."

"Why, many hold Giuseppe's violins
As good as thine."
"May be: they are different.
His quality declines: he spoils his hand
With over-drinking. But were his the best,
He could not work for two. My work is mine,
And, heresy or not, if my hand slacked,
I should rob God — since He is fullest good —
Leaving a blank instead of violins.
I say, not God Himself can make man's best
Without best men to help Him. I am one best
Here in Cremona, using sunlight well
To fashion finest maple till it serves
More cunningly than throats, for harmony.
'Tis rare delight: I would not change my skill
To be the Emperor with bungling hands,
And lose my work, which comes as natural
As self at waking."

"Thou art little more
Than a deft potter's wheel, Antonio;
Turning out work by mere necessity
And lack of varied function. Higher arts
Subsist on freedom — eccentricity —
Uncounted inspirations — influence
That comes with drinking, gambling, talk turned
wild,
Then moody misery and lack of food —
With every dithyrambic fine excess:
These make at last a storm which flashes out
In lighting revelations. Steady work
Turns genius to a loom; the soul must lie
Like grapes beneath the sun till ripeness comes
And mellow vintage. I could paint you now
The finest Crucifixion; yesterday
Returning home I saw it on a sky
Blue-black, thick-starred. I want two louis d'ors
To buy the canvas and the costly blues —
Trust me a fortnight."

"Where are those last two
I lent thee for thy Judith?—her thou saw'st

In saffron gown, with Holofernes' head
And beauty all complete?"
"She is but sketched:
I lack the proper model — and the mood.
A great idea is an eagle's egg,
Craves time for hatching; while the eagle sits
Feed her."
"If thou wilt call thy pictures eggs
I call the hatching, work. 'Tis God gives skill,
But not without men's hands: He could not make
Antonio Stradivari's violins
Without Antonio. Get thee to thy easel."

1873.

TWO LOVERS.

TWO LOVERS.

Two lovers by a moss-grown spring:
  They leaned soft cheeks together there,
  Mingled the dark and sunny hair,
And heard the wooing thrushes sing.
          O budding time!
          O love's blest prime!

Two wedded from the portal stept:
  The bells made happy carollings,
  The air was soft as fanning wings,
White petals on the pathway slept.
          O pure-eyed bride!
          O tender pride!

Two faces o'er a cradle bent:
  Two hands above the head were locked;
  These pressed each other while they rocked,
Those watched a life that love had sent.
  O solemn hour!
  O hidden power!

Two parents by the evening fire:
  The red light fell about their knees
  On heads that rose by slow degrees
Like buds upon the lily spire.
  O patient life!
  O tender strife!

The two still sat together there,
  The red light shone about their knees;
  But all the heads by slow degrees
Had gone and left that lonely pair.
  O voyage fast!
  O vanished past!

The red light shone upon the floor
  And made the space between them wide;
  They drew their chairs up side by side,
Their pale cheeks joined, and said, "Once more!"
O memories!
O past that is!

1866.

ARION.

ARION.

(Herod. I. 24.)

Arion, whose melodic soul
Taught the dithyramb to roll
Like forest fires, and sing
Olympian suffering,

Had carried his diviner lore
From Corinth to the sister shore
Where Greece could largelier be,
Branching o'er Italy.

Then weighted with his glorious name
And bags of gold, aboard he came
'Mid harsh seafaring men
To Corinth bound again.

The sailors eyed the bags, and thought
" The gold is good, the man is nought—
And who shall track the wave
That opens for his grave?"

With brawny arms and cruel eyes
They press around him where he lies
In sleep beside his lyre,
Hearing the Muses choir.

He waked and saw this wolf-faced Death
Breaking the dream that filled his breath
With inspiration strong
Of yet unchanted song.

"Take, take my gold and let me live!"
He prayed, as kings do when they give
Their all with royal will,
Holding born kingship still.

To rob the living they refuse,
One death or other he must choose,
Either the watery pall
Or wounds and burial.

"My solemn robe then let me don,
Give me high space to stand upon,
That dying I may pour
A song unsung before."

It pleased them well to grant this prayer,
To hear for nought how it might fare
With men who paid their gold
For what a poet sold.

In flowing stole, his eyes aglow
With inward fire, he neared the prow
And took his god-like stand,
The cithara in hand.

The wolfish men all shrank aloof,
And feared this singer might be proof
Against their murderous power,
After his lyric hour.

But he, in liberty of song,
Fearless of death or other wrong,
With full spondaic toll
Poured forth his mighty soul:

Poured forth the strain his dream had taught,
A nome with lofty passion fraught,
Such as makes battles won
On fields of Marathon.

The last long vowels trembled then
As awe within those wolfish men:
        They said, with mutual stare,
        Some god was present there.

But lo! Arion leaped on high
Ready, his descant done, to die;
        Not asking, "Is it well?"
        Like a pierced eagle fell.

1873.

"O MAY I JOIN THE CHOIR INVISIBLE."

"O MAY I JOIN THE CHOIR INVISIBLE."

"*Longum illud tempus, quum non ero, magis me movet, quam hoc exiguum.*"—CICERO, ad Att., xii. 18.

O MAY I join the choir invisible
Of those immortal dead who live again
In minds made better by their presence: live
In pulses stirred to generosity,
In deeds of daring rectitude, in scorn
For miserable aims that end with self,
In thoughts sublime that pierce the night like stars,
And with their mild persistence urge man's search
To vaster issues.
So to live is heaven:
To make undying music in the world,

Breathing as beauteous order that controls
With growing sway the growing life of man.
So we inherit that sweet purity
For which we struggled, failed, and agonized
With widening retrospect that bred despair.
Rebellious flesh that would not be subdued,
A vicious parent shaming still its child
Poor anxious penitence, is quick dissolved;
Its discords, quenched by meeting harmonies,
Die in the large and charitable air.
And all our rarer, better, truer self,
That sobbed religiously in yearning song,
That watched to ease the burthen of the world,
Laboriously tracing what must be,
And what may yet be better — saw within
A worthier image for the sanctuary,
And shaped it forth before the multitude
Divinely human, raising worship so
To higher reverence more mixed with love —
That better self shall live till human Time
Shall fold its eyelids, and the human sky
Be gathered like a scroll within the tomb
Unread forever.

This is life to come,
Which martyred men have made more glorious
For us who strive to follow. May I reach
That purest heaven, be to other souls
The cup of strength in some great agony,
Enkindle generous ardor, feed pure love,
Beget the smiles that have no cruelty —
Be the sweet presence of a good diffused,
And in diffusion ever more intense.
So shall I join the choir invisible
Whose music is the gladness of the world.

1867.

THE END.

www.ingramcontent.com/pod-product-compliance
Lightning Source LLC
LaVergne TN
LVHW012327100826
845148LV00017B/393